THE SCOPES MONKEY TRIAL

A Headline Court Case

Headline Court Cases

The Andersonville Prison Civil War Crimes Trial
A Headline Court Case
0-7660-1386-3

The John Brown Slavery Revolt Trial
A Headline Court Case
0-7660-1385-5

The Lindbergh Baby Kidnapping Trial
A Headline Court Case
0-7660-1389-8

The Lizzie Borden "Axe Murder" Trial
A Headline Court Case
0-7660-1422-3

The Nuremberg Nazi War Crimes Trials
A Headline Court Case
0-7660-1384-7

The Sacco and Vanzetti Controversial Murder Trial
A Headline Court Case
0-7660-1387-1

The Salem Witchcraft Trials
A Headline Court Case
0-7660-1383-9

The Scopes Monkey Trial
A Headline Court Case
0-7660-1388-X

THE SCOPES MONKEY TRIAL

A Headline Court Case

Freya Ottem Hanson

Enslow Publishers, Inc.

40 Industrial Road	PO Box 38
Box 398	Aldershot
Berkeley Heights, NJ 07922	Hants GU12 6BP
USA	UK

http://www.enslow.com

For a friend and encourager, Janet French

Library of Congress Cataloging-in-Publication Data

Hanson, Freya Ottem, 1949–
  The Scopes monkey trial : a headline court case / Freya Ottem Hanson.
    p. cm. — (Headline court cases)
  Includes bibliographical references and index.
  Summary: Discusses one of the most famous court cases in history, in
  which a Tennessee high school teacher was put on trial for teaching
  evolution.
  ISBN 0-7660-1388-X
  1. Scopes, John Thomas—Trials, litigation, etc.—Juvenile literature.
  2. Evolution—Study and teaching—Law
  and legislation—Tennessee—Juvenile literature. [1. Scopes, John
  Thomas—Trials, litigation, etc. 2. Evolution—Study and teaching—Law
  and legislation.] I. Title. II. Series.
  KF224.S3 H36 2000
  345.73'0287—dc21
                                    99-050503

Printed in the United States of America

10 9 8 7 6 5 4 3 2

To Our Readers: All Internet addresses in this book were active and appropriate
when we went to press. Any comments or suggestions can be sent by e-mail to
Comments@enslow.com or to the address on the back cover.

Photo Credits: Courtesy of Bryan College, pp. 3, 8, 11, 12, 26, 29, 30, 33, 39,
45, 49, 51 (both), 59, 62, 64, 67, 72, 81, 83, 86, 93, 106; Library of Congress,
pp. 16, 35, 42, 47.

Cover Photo: Courtesy of Bryan College

Contents

chapter one

A COURT OR A CIRCUS?

DAYTON, TN—Cardboard monkeys appeared in store windows. Merchants sold souvenir cotton toy monkeys on sticks. Pins read, "Your Old Man's a Monkey," and live chimpanzees came to perform.

Dayton, Tennessee, 1925

The atmosphere in Dayton, Tennessee, during the summer of 1925 seemed more like a circus than the setting of a trial. But John Thomas Scopes, a twenty-four-year-old teacher, was indeed standing trial for teaching evolution at Rhea County Central High School. He was not surprised, though, when he was arrested for teaching this theory in the classroom. The first-year teacher had agreed with local businesspeople to be part of a case to test a Tennessee law. The law known as the Butler Act had been passed by Tennessee lawmakers, and Governor Peay of Tennessee had signed it into law on March 21, 1925. This law made teaching evolution illegal in the public schools. It read as follows:

. . . that it shall be unlawful for any teacher in any of the universities, . . . and all other public schools of the state, which are supported in whole or in part by the public school funds of the state, to teach any theory that denies the story of the Divine creation of man as taught in the Bible, and to teach instead that man has descended from a lower order of animals.[1]

The American Civil Liberties Union (ACLU), a national organization founded in 1920 that sought to protect individual freedoms such as freedom of speech, placed an ad in the *Chattanooga Daily News*. The ACLU offered to cover the costs for a teacher who would be willing to challenge the Tennessee law. Several Dayton businesspeople read the offer and thought a trial might bring some publicity to their town

Teenage girls on the courthouse lawn show their monkey doll souvenirs that were being sold during the Scopes *trial. This was only one of the many ways the community of Dayton, Tennessee, tried to promote what has been called the "trial of the century."*

of eighteen hundred people. These people then agreed to ask John Scopes, a high school teacher who had substituted for the biology teacher, to be a part of the plan. Scopes agreed and showed the businesspeople the textbook he had used, George William Hunter's *A Civic Biology*. The textbook, approved and used in many Tennessee public schools, included Darwin's theory of evolution, a theory that claimed all life came from a single organism.

Darwin's theory was not well received among people who believed in fundamentalism. The members of this movement insist that the words of the Bible be taken literally. They concluded that Darwin's explanation of Creation opposed the story of Creation found in the first book of the Bible, Genesis. They urged the lawmakers in several states to pass laws that prohibited teaching Darwin's theory in the schools. The fundamentalist movement successfully convinced Tennessee lawmakers to approve an antievolution law.

The merchants of Dayton, not willing to pass up an opportunity to have this trial in their hometown, persuaded local authorities to prosecute, or press charges against, John Scopes. They organized the trial, welcomed the lawyers on both sides, and even painted the courthouse for the event. But they could not have imagined the publicity the trial would receive.

The *Scopes* trial was the first American trial ever to be broadcast on radio. Station WGN from Chicago installed microphones in the courtroom and picked up the proceedings. Hundreds of journalists poured into the town, and telegraph operators tapped out millions of words that would circulate around the world. Reporters from several European countries, unassisted by the convenience of modern air travel, made the long journey to Dayton. Motion picture photographers positioned their cameras for action.

Reporters, taking off on the idea that Darwin's theory claimed people descended from the monkey, named the event the Scopes Monkey Trial. The "monkey" theme stuck. Robinson's Drugstore sold a fifteen-cent soda drink called a Monkey Fizz. Stuffed monkey dolls were even sold as souvenirs.

Dayton not only decorated its storefronts with monkey signs and posters, but also put up religious posters. Citizens strung a banner that said, "Read Your Bible," across the outside of the Rhea County Courthouse, where the trial was held. Other signs, such as, "Come to Jesus" and "Prepare to meet Thy Maker," hung from utility poles.

Food vendors lined the streets and sold lemonade, hot dogs, ice cream, soda, corn bread, and watermelon. Booksellers set up stands. The Anti-Evolution League sold T. T. Martin's best-selling book, *Hell and the High School*, and several books by William Jennings Bryan, an antievolutionist, three-time presidential candidate, and one of the best-known lawyers in the trial.

Ministers preached from street corners and in tents. Religious meetings were common and curiosity-seeking farmers and miners from the surrounding countryside came to watch the religious showdown. The courtroom, which held fewer than a thousand people, could not hold the many who flocked to Dayton, Tennessee. The courtroom's limited space did not, however, seem to stop the flow of people who came to see the forces of religion take on what was called "godless science."

The merchants of Dayton could not have imagined the publicity this trial would bring to their town located forty miles north of Chattanooga. Almost from the moment of the announcement that the trial would be held in Dayton, a carnival-like atmosphere prevailed. The atmosphere,

The Scopes *trial became known as the "Monkey Trial" because of an interpretation of Darwin's theory that contended that man descended from the ape. In another town promotion, chimpanzee Joe Mindy drinks a "Monkey Fizz" at the local drugstore.*

however, was not the only thing that held the attention of so many citizens, nor what attracted two famous lawyers—William Jennings Bryan and Clarence Darrow—to the sweltering heat of Dayton in July 1925.

So what was at stake? The trial did not involve a famous murder or kidnapping or even a serious crime against the government. There were no famous arrests or searches for a criminal. In fact, the defendant, John Scopes, was a willing participant in a trial that still draws attention some seventy-five years later.

John Scopes, Dr. John R. Neal, one of Scopes's attorneys, and George Rappleyea, the original trial planner (from left to right), walk under a "Read Your Bible" sign in Dayton, Tennessee, a statement that was supported by the majority of the townspeople.

The trial did establish two groups of people. The first group wanted control of how their tax dollars were spent on education, and they did not want Darwin's theory of evolution taught. The other group wanted to apply the First Amendment right to freedom of speech, and that included what was taught in school classrooms.

The *Scopes* case is essentially a case that cuts across two First Amendment lines: the right of free speech and the Establishment Clause, which prohibits the state from promoting any particular religious view.

Was this simply a trial to determine what should be taught in schools or was there more at stake? What exactly did the First Amendment mean when it said, "Congress shall make no law respecting an establishment of religion, or prohibiting the free exercise thereof; or abridging the freedom of speech . . .?"[2]

chapter two

DARWIN AND THE FUNDAMENTALISTS

ENGLAND—What caused all of the commotion that resulted in the 1925 *Scopes* trial? To find out, let's go back to 1859. That year in Great Britain, a naturalist (one who studies plants and animal life) by the name of Charles R. Darwin (1809–1882) published a controversial book called *The Origin of Species By Means of Natural Selection of Favoured Races in the Struggle for Life*. In this work, he presented the theory that plants and animals come from a few common ancestors and have evolved and changed gradually over millions of years. Darwin said this evolutionary process came about by "natural selection."

Born in Shrewsbury, England, Darwin studied at the University of Edinburgh in Scotland, and Cambridge University in England. His botany teacher recommended him for a voyage. After his graduation in 1831, twenty-two-year-old Darwin boarded a ship known as the H.M.S. *Beagle*. He set sail as an unpaid naturalist with the crew on a five-year trip around the world.

On that voyage, Darwin

continued his lifetime pursuit of collecting scientific data. In September 1835, the voyage of the *Beagle* brought the crew to the Galapagos Islands. This group of fifteen large and many smaller islands located about five hundred miles west of Ecuador, South America, in the Pacific Ocean, was known for its varieties of plants and animals. Tortoises that weighed more than five hundred pounds and iguanas that grew to over four feet lived on the islands. These remarkable animals caught Darwin's attention.

For several weeks, Darwin traveled from island to island of the Galapagos. He noted certain differences in the biology on each island. On one of the islands, where only insects were available for food, finches had small beaks. On another island, where the finches had to break open seeds to survive, their beaks were larger and more powerful. Darwin concluded that these birds, although they had a common ancestor, had evolved or changed to survive in different environments. He later concluded that humans had evolved as well. This theory became known as Darwin's theory of evolution.

But what was the reaction to Darwin's theory? Charles Lyell, an English geologist (one who studies the composition, structure, and origin of rocks), wrote to Darwin after the publication of the book, "I have just finished your volume. . . . It is a splendid case of close reasoning . . . with my hearty congratulations to you on your grand work, believe me."[1]

Darwin was concerned about public opinion and especially wanted to convince well-known English biologist

In 1859, Charles Darwin published Origin of Species, *which held the theory that man evolved from a lower form of animals. This work led to laws that banned the teaching of evolution in public schools. The state of Tennessee passed the Butler Act that became the subject of the* Scopes *trial in 1925.*

Thomas Huxley of this theory. Huxley's approval was obtained much more easily than Darwin might have thought. Huxley not only agreed with Darwin, but said, "Nothing, I think, can be better than the tone of the book. . . . As for your doctrine, I am prepared to go the stake."[2]

In 1871, Darwin wrote *The Descent of Man*. This book presented the theory that humans descended from a primitive organism that adapted to its environment. According to Darwin, the ability of humans to change and adapt made it possible for them to survive.

Darwin must have thought people in both the scientific and religious fields would oppose him. He wrote in the conclusion of his *The Origin of Species*:

> Although I am fully convinced of the truth of the views given in this volume . . . I by no means expect to convince experienced naturalists . . . from a point of view directly opposite to mine. It is so easy to hide our ignorance under such expressions of the "plan of creation" and "unity of design."[3]

Darwin must have been surprised how quickly his ideas convinced not only the scientific world, but also many religious leaders. By the turn of the century, many scientists accepted Darwin's theory of evolution. Religious leaders, known as modernists, also incorporated the theory into their religious teachings. They no longer asked church members to believe that the earth was created in six days as the Genesis account said.

By 1925, the year of the *Scopes* trial, Darwin's theory of evolution had become a part of the regular curriculum in public schools in Europe and the United States. Hunter's *A Civic Biology*, the textbook used in the class John Scopes taught in Dayton, Tennessee, also included Darwin's theory.[4]

Yet, Darwin's views troubled many. Some students of the Bible believed Darwin's theories opposed the account of Creation found in Genesis. They said that animals, including people, were created in a single day, and that humans descended from one man and one woman. Some stretched Darwin's theory and claimed Darwin said people came from the monkey, something Darwin himself did not say. Those who opposed Darwin's theory were convinced that they must stop this theory from being taught in the public schools. This group came to follow the principles of fundamentalism.

Darwin's Theory Challenged

The fundamentalist movement took on the name of a set of pamphlets that were known as "The Fundamentals—Testimony to the Truth." These pamphlets were written and published between 1910 and 1915 in the United States. Two wealthy founders of Union Oil Company published them and sent them to leaders in Christian churches and organizations in the English-speaking world. These works set forth many of the basic beliefs of the movement. Several of these beliefs were as follows:

1. Christ was born to a virgin.

2. Jesus Christ was God.

3. Jesus rose from the dead.

4. The death of Jesus paid for all sins.

5. Jesus is coming again.

6. The Bible is trustworthy and accurate.

Fundamentalism taught that the theory of evolution (some called it *evil-lution*) discredited the accuracy of the Bible by tampering with the account of Creation as found in the first two chapters of Genesis. One challenger of the theory of evolution wrote, "The evidence for evolution, even in its milder form, does not begin to be as strong as that for the revelation of God in the Bible."[5]

Another article in this collection had this warning for ministers who supported evolution:

> And yet there are ministers of the Gospel who, discrediting the Bible narrative of creation, are still basing argument upon the Darwinian Theory of the Origin of Species—referring to the time when our ancestors were dwelling in trees, descending from monkeys, tadpoles and fish.[6]

Concerned about the teaching of evolution in the schools, another follower of the fundamentalist movement wrote, "The teaching of Darwinism as an approved science, to the children and youth of the schools of the world is the most deplorable feature of the whole wretched propaganda."[7]

Fundamentalism gained in popularity among some clergy and many ordinary citizens. Although the movement did not begin a separate denomination, fundamentalism existed in many Christian denominations, such as Methodist, Baptist, and Presbyterian. The movement was especially popular in rural areas and in the South, although support for fundamentalist beliefs existed throughout the country.

In 1919, Dr. William Bell Riley, a minister of a large church in Minneapolis, Minnesota, started the World Christian Fundamentals Association. He believed that Christians should actively address the problems of the world—and one of those troubling areas was evolution.

The 1920s were complex times. The Nineteenth Amendment to the United States Constitution was passed in 1920, and women were, for the first time in this country, granted the right to vote. Nellie Ross of Wyoming became the nation's first female governor. Lawrence Welk started his musical group, and Louis Armstrong and Duke Ellington recorded jazz. In 1927 Charles Lindbergh became an international figure when he made the first nonstop flight across the Atlantic. People huddled around the radio to hear comedy hours and listen to political speeches. Listening to the radio was fast becoming the national pastime. Education also changed in the 1920s. Thousands of students, who would previously have only received a few years of public education, attended and were expected to complete high school. And in those very schools, the theory of evolution was taught.

The World Christian Fundamentals Association (WCFA) was concerned about the widespread exposure this theory was getting. As a result, the organization encouraged lawmakers to pass bills that made it illegal to teach the theory of evolution in the public schools.

Darwin's Challengers Take Their Cause to the Lawmakers

Those who believed in fundamentalism needed a champion for their cause, and they soon found one in three-time presidential candidate William Jennings Bryan from Salem, Illinois. Bryan enjoyed talking not only about politics, but also about his favorite subject—the Bible. He supported the antievolution cause in America. And he did not back down easily. It was reported that "by 1925, Bryan and his followers had succeeded in getting laws introduced in fifteen states [including Tennessee] to ban the teaching of evolution."[8]

In the early 1920s, efforts were made in South Carolina, Kentucky, Florida, and Texas to introduce laws banning the teaching of Darwin's theories in the public schools. In these states, the efforts demonstrated an antievolution trend. Although these laws did not get approved, in Kentucky the proposed law failed by only one vote in the House of Representatives. In Florida, a nonbinding resolution (one that could not be enforced as law) that urged teachers not to teach evolution passed both the house and senate.[9]

In 1923 alone, antievolution bills were introduced in six states. Oklahoma passed a law that banned textbooks that had evolutionary material. The following year, even though an antievolution bill failed to pass, Oklahoma school officials removed from schools all biology books that taught Darwin's theory of evolution.

Another antievolution leader emerged. In Tennessee, John Washington Butler, a wealthy farmer, campaigned against evolution in his election bid for a seat in the Tennessee House of Representatives.[10] Butler later recalled, "I wrote it [the bill] out after breakfast at home just like I wanted it. . . . Ninety-nine people out of a hundred in my district thought just as I did." The bill passed both the House and Senate. The House of Representatives passed the bill seventy-five to five and the Senate twenty-four to six.[11] All they needed was the governor's signature.

On March 21, 1925, Governor Austin Peay signed the Butler Act forbidding the teaching of evolution in the public schools of Tennessee. Tennessee became the first state to have an antievolution law. The governor doubted the law would get much attention, and even said, "Nobody believes that it is going to be an active statute."[12] He did not realize just how much attention the Butler Act would get.

chapter three

ROBINSON'S DRUGSTORE

UNITED STATES—The 1920s were a time of changes in the United States. For the first time in the history of this country, more people lived in cities than on farms. The radio, car, telephone, and even household appliances such as the washing machine had become part of life.

Following World War I (1914–1918), the first war that American soldiers fought on foreign land, life in America changed dramatically. Many women began working outside the home, and some women began wearing new styles of clothing. The short skirt replaced the long dress. With automobiles, which more people owned, people were able to drive to the movies, baseball games, and places called speakeasies, where they could listen to jazz music and dance the Charleston.

Right in the middle of this decade, the *Scopes* trial made headlines, putting Dayton, Tennessee, on the map. The controversial case began at Robinson's Drugstore, the place where local businesspeople got together.

On May 4, 1925, a

notice appeared in the *Chattanooga Daily News* in which an American Civil Liberties Union (ACLU) press release was quoted as follows:

> We are looking for a Tennessee teacher who is willing to accept our services in testing this law [the Tennessee law prohibiting the teaching of evolution in public schools] in the courts. Our lawyers think a friendly test case can be arranged without costing a teacher his or her job. Distinguished counsel have volunteered their services. All we need now is a willing client. By this test we hope to render a real service to freedom of teaching through the country, for we do not believe the law will be sustained.[1]

The American Civil Liberties Union, established in 1920, sought to protect the constitutional rights of individuals. Roger Baldwin founded the organization at a time when citizens were jailed for opposing war, the races were segregated, and violence against African Americans was not unusual. The ACLU believed that the government should be limited in its control of what people could say and do. It supported the rights found in the first ten amendments to the United States Constitution, known as the Bill of Rights. The organization provided legal advice for individuals and groups willing to challenge certain laws or conduct.[2] The Butler Act was especially offensive to this group. In fact, the ACLU had been following the passage of this Tennessee law and wanted it thrown out, but it needed a willing teacher to see it through.

Forty miles north of Chattanooga, George W. Rappleyea, the thirty-one-year-old manager of the bankrupt Cumberland Coal and Iron Company, read the paper with interest. His troubled and declining coal company had seen better days, and he was looking for ways to promote local business. In the 1870s, Dayton's population had stood at four thousand people. By 1925, only eighteen hundred people lived in Dayton, and the coal mines were all but abandoned.

Rappleyea, a New Yorker with an engineering degree, had come to Dayton three years before. On a trip to the Appalachian Mountains, a snake bit him, and he ended up marrying the nurse who took care of him at a hospital in nearby Athens.[3]

Although Rappleyea was Christian and attended a Methodist church, he was not a follower of fundamentalism. He favored evolution, and in that respect, his views differed from most of the residents of Dayton. Most people in Dayton held to a strict Christianity that opposed Darwin's theory of how life began.

H. L. Mencken, a famed reporter of the *Scopes* trial, described the town as pleasant but too moral for him.[4] He longed for a merry laugh and a burst of happy music. In many ways, Dayton was far from backward. A quiet town in the Cumberland Mountains, this town had lovely homes, two banks, and several factories. A hotel stood on Main Street as did Robinson's Drugstore, the social gathering place of the town. Medicines, books, magazines, sporting goods, and even school textbooks were sold there. Citizens stopped to sit at the soda fountain and sip sodas.

Rappleyea came to Robinson's Drugstore on May 4, hoping to attract business investors to Dayton. He wanted to discuss his latest idea—a trial in Dayton. And this would not be just any trial. It would be one that would draw attention. Robinson's Drugstore was the place where many gathered to discuss the weather and local politics. The owner, Frank Earle Robinson, who called himself the Hustling Druggist, agreed that a trial might bring some attention to their city. Robinson was chairman of the Rhea County School Board, and there, within arm's reach on his own store shelves, stood the controversial textbook, Hunter's *A Civic Biology*.[5]

The next day, May 5, several other businesspeople,

Robinson's Drugstore became a popular spot during the trial, where people gathered to get news from out-of-town papers or to get out of the unbearable summer heat.

attorneys, and school officials met at Robinson's Drugstore to talk about the possible case. Although accounts differ about who was present, most accounts agree that in addition to Rappleyea and Robinson, who was chairman of the school board, at least five others were involved. They included the superintendent of schools, Walter White, and three local attorneys.[6]

Those who met at Robinson's Drugstore held different views on evolution, but they all agreed that a trial might be just the thing Dayton needed. They were not about to let go of this opportunity. What the enterprising businesspeople needed was a teacher who would stand trial. School had ended for the year. W. F. Ferguson, the high school biology teacher, refused to be involved. As a result, the attention centered on a single, twenty-four-year-old teacher who had just completed his first year of teaching at the Rhea County Central High School. His name was John Thomas Scopes.

The drugstore group asked a young boy sitting at the soda fountain to find John Scopes. The boy located the teacher at a tennis court and asked him to come to the drugstore. Scopes, still sweaty from his tennis game, had no idea what the request would be. At the drugstore, when asked about the possibility of a test case, Scopes hesitated. He was the football, basketball, and baseball coach, and had taught math, physics, and chemistry, but not biology. But he had substituted for the regular biology teacher, who had become ill in the spring. Scopes had reviewed the textbook with the students. He could not recall whether or not he had actually taught the section on evolution to the class, but agreed to help with the case.[7] Some accounts say Scopes gave some students a quick lesson on evolution before the July trial, just so lawyers could say he had actually taught the subject. Dayton now had their teacher.

Scopes got a copy of Hunter's *A Civic Biology* from the shelves in the drugstore, and showed the pages on evolution to those who were present. The book praised the work of Darwin in these words:

> The great English scientist, Charles Darwin, from this and other evidence, explained the theory of evolution. This is the belief that simple forms of life on earth slowly and gradually gave rise to those more complex and that thus ultimately the most complex forms came into existence. . . . His life should mean to us not so much the association of his name with the *Origin of Species* . . . but rather that of a patient, courteous, and brave gentleman who struggled with true English pluck against the odds of disease and the attacks of hostile critics. He gave the world the proofs of the theory on which we today base the progress of the world.[8]

Scopes left the store and went to finish his tennis game. Rappleyea left the drugstore with another purpose in mind. He walked to the telegraph office and sent the following telegram to the American Civil Liberties Union:

AMERICAN CIVIL LIBERTIES UNION, 100 FIFTH AVENUE, NEW YORK

J.T. SCOPES, TEACHER OF SCIENCE RHEA COUNTY HIGH SCHOOL, DAYTON, TENN., WILL BE ARRESTED AND CHARGED WITH TEACHING EVOLUTION. CONSENT OF SUPERINTENDENT OF EDUCATION FOR TEST CASE TO BE DEFENDED

BY YOU. WIRE ME COLLECT IF YOU WISH TO CO-
OPERATE AND REST WILL FOLLOW.

G. W. RAPPLEYEA[9]

The next afternoon, May 6, Rappleyea came to the drugstore with a telegram in reply from the ACLU. It said that
they would cooperate with financial help, legal advice, and
publicity. Rappleyea sent another telegram to the ACLU in

*The Dayton trial planners meeting at the local drugstore are, seated
from left: Herb Hicks, attorney for the prosecution; John Scopes; Walter
White, superintendent of Schools; Gordon McKenzie, attorney for the
prosecution. Standing from left: Burt Wilbur, warrant server; Wallace
Haggard, attorney for the prosecution; W. E. Morgan, businessman;
George Rappleyea, business manager and trial planner; Sue Hicks,
attorney for the prosecution; and F. E. Robinson, drugstore owner.*

which he indicated that a warrant for Scopes's arrest would be issued.

In order to accommodate the arrest, Scopes volunteered to have Burt Wilbur serve him the necessary papers. Scopes was handed the warrant outside Robinson's Drugstore, and told to appear on Saturday, May 9, before three justices of the peace of Rhea County. On May 9, Rappleyea and Scopes both appeared before the justices. Rappleyea showed the justices a copy of the Butler Act and the portions on evolution in Hunter's *A Civic Biology* used in the class Scopes

Local businesspeople planned Dayton's involvement in testing the Butler Act. They also hoped that the town would benefit financially from the Scopes *trial.*

taught. Scopes was released on bond, a sum of money that granted him freedom from jail until the time of the trial, but guaranteed his return at trial. The next step was to get the grand jury to issue an indictment, a formal charge, against Scopes. They were not scheduled to meet until August.[10]

Dayton businesspeople were uneasy about waiting that long. Would someone else beat them to the punch and schedule a trial? In the middle of May, the Dayton business-people's fears were confirmed. Chattanooga leaders tried to get the *Scopes* trial moved to their Memorial Auditorium. When they were turned down, they attempted to set up their own test case against their own teacher.

The Dayton businesspeople countered. They called for Scopes to return from Kentucky where he was on vacation. Judge John Raulston scheduled a special meeting of the grand jury, and on May 25, 1925, an indictment, a charge of a crime worthy of trial, was issued. Instead of August, Dayton had managed to schedule the trial of the *State of Tennessee* v. *John Thomas Scopes* for July 10, 1925.

chapter four

JOHN SCOPES AND THE ANTI-EVOLUTION ACT

DAYTON, TN—When John Thomas Scopes came to teach at the high school in Dayton, Tennessee, he could not have realized that less than a year later he would become the center of a storm. Although that storm about teaching evolution in the schools had been on the horizon for several years, it would culminate in an eight-day trial in Dayton, Tennessee, in July 1925.

Who was this shy, twenty-four-year-old, red-haired defendant who had to tell his father not to brag so much during the trial? The fifth child and only son of Thomas Scopes and Mary Alva Brown, John Scopes was born on August 3, 1900, in Paducah, Kentucky, a town of some twenty thousand people, along the Ohio River. His father had come from England to America in 1860 and was hired on the railroads as a mechanic. Scopes's father supported the labor unions at a time in our country's history when such unions had little power. Labor unions represented the workers and sought to improve working conditions for employees. When these

In his first year as a high school teacher, twenty-four-year old John T. Scopes agreed to test the validity of the Butler Act. After the trial, he never taught again.

groups first became a part of American life, workers were still working long days, six or seven days a week. They were given no vacation time, no overtime pay, poor pay, no holidays, and no health insurance benefits.

Scopes's father became involved in the Pullman Strike of 1894. The Pullman Strike involved workers who refused to work at the company that made railroad cars with beds, or sleeper cars known as Pullmans. The American Railway Union (ARU) supported the workers and ordered its members not to move Pullman cars. The strike (work stoppage) eventually became violent and railroad property was destroyed. Eugene Debs, the spokesman for the ARU, was arrested and Clarence Darrow became his lawyer. From that time on, Darrow was thought to be sympathetic to workers. Clarence Darrow later became the attorney for John Scopes. Scopes's mother, Mary Alva Brown, was the granddaughter of a minister who started many of the Presbyterian churches in western Kentucky.

Because of his father's work, John Scopes moved several times as a child. At the age of seven, he moved with his family from Paducah, Kentucky, to Danville, Illinois. Two years later the family moved to Salem, Illinois, the hometown of William Jennings Bryan. Because of his connection with the town, Bryan was a familiar speaker at graduation ceremonies in Salem. Before they met in Dayton, John Scopes was already acquainted with Bryan, who had been his high school graduation speaker. Scopes entered the University of Illinois in Urbana in 1919. The following spring, he came down with a severe case of bronchitis, a swelling of small tubes in the lungs that can result in severe fits of coughing, and was sent home. Hoping a warmer climate would be more to his liking, Scopes transferred to the University of Kentucky in Lexington, but the illness persisted, and again, Scopes was forced to quit school. When his health was finally restored, Scopes returned to school, and took classes that interested him, like law, geology, mathematics, and zoology. Unfortunately the combination of classes did not allow him to graduate, so he was forced to rearrange his schedule and work very hard to get the credits necessary to graduate in the spring of 1924. Scopes earned

John Scopes's father, Thomas Scopes (right), who read Darwin's works to his son (left), attended the trial in Dayton.

a Bachelor of Arts degree in law, the first time the University of Kentucky had awarded that degree.

Short of money, Scopes was prompted to find a teaching job. The football coach at Central High in Dayton had resigned unexpectedly, and the school was left without a coach or teacher of algebra, physics, and chemistry. John Scopes was offered the teaching position. His pay would be one hundred fifty dollars a month, and the job would run from September 1, 1924, to May 1, 1925. With no other job offers in sight, Scopes took the position and moved to Dayton. The town welcomed the young coach and teacher. Scopes recalled that year with fondness. "I had pleasant memories and a windfall of friendships that survived the decades."[1]

The Bailey family offered Scopes a room in their house, even though they were well-off and probably did not need to take in boarders. (Bailey ran the largest hardware store in the region.) Scopes also got to know George W. Rappleyea, the manager of the Cumberland Coal and Iron Co., and even attended parties in his home on a couple of occasions. When the two sat down at Robinson's Drugstore to discuss a potential trial, they already knew each other.

When school ended on May 1, 1925, Scopes intended to return to Paducah, Kentucky, to sell Ford automobiles for the summer. In the meantime, he met a young lady he wanted to get to know. She had informed him that her church was sponsoring a social, but he never got the opportunity to go.[2] The meeting at Robinson's Drugstore intervened.

Scopes later described what happened.

> On a warm May afternoon, four days after the term was over, I was playing tennis on the old outdoor clay court at school with some of my students . . . in the middle of our game, a little boy walked up and watched us smack the ball back and forth. He was waiting for me, and when we had finished a point, he called, "Mr. Scopes?" I nodded and trotted over to him.[3]

Inside the drugstore, Scopes sat down and sipped on a soda. Doc Robinson came straight to the point: "John, we've been arguing, and I said that nobody could teach biology without teaching evolution."[4] Scopes agreed with what the local businessman said. Then Scopes picked up a copy of *A Civic Biology* from a nearby shelf. It had been used as an official textbook in Tennessee schools since 1919. Scopes showed it to those who gathered. Apparently Butler, who had written the law, did not even realize that evolution had been approved for use in Tennessee schools for several years.[5]

Then the group asked Scopes if he would be willing to stand trial for teaching evolution in the classroom. The regular biology teacher, W. F. Ferguson, had already turned them down. Scopes believed in the case. He thought the Butler Act (antievolution law) was a bad one that should be overturned. Later in life, Scopes reflected on the decision that he made:

> If I had been the regular biology teacher at Rhea County Central High School I wouldn't have let the law restrict my teaching the truth. How could I have, considering my environmental influences? My father had read to me from

Charles Darwin's *Origin of Species*, [and] *Descent of Man* . . . which I had then finished reading for myself . . . I thought Darwin was right. It was the only plausible explanation of man's long and tortuous journey to his present physical and mental development.[6]

Scopes never could have imagined the attention the trial would draw. When he said he would be involved, he must have thought the trial would be a rather quiet matter in Dayton, just among friends. It grew to far more than a simple matter. But in all of the commotion, the trial *did* ignore John Scopes. As one historian said, "Once Dayton was inundated by celebrities, Scopes himself was forgotten. . . . He attended the proceedings only to be ignored."[7]

The American Civil Liberties Union made decisions as though John Scopes did not exist. Lawyers Darrow and Bryan drew most of the attention of the media; Scopes spoke only once during the entire eight-day trial. Yet this reserved twenty-four-year-old teacher became the center of the storm that swept Dayton the summer of 1925, and it is the name of Scopes that is remembered.

John Scopes became involved in a whirlwind of activity that included trips to New York City to meet with defense attorneys. Although the American Civil Liberties Union was reluctant to have Clarence Darrow involved, Scopes finally said he wanted the team of Clarence Darrow and Dudley Field Malone to represent him. William Jennings Bryan had already joined the team of prosecutors, and Scopes became convinced he needed someone trained in difficult courtroom trials to be his lawyer. Darrow was his choice, and he did not regret that decision. Scopes reminded the ACLU that Bryan himself would turn the trial into a free-for-all and that Darrow was best equipped for a tough battle.[8]

As part of the pretrial strategy, Scopes asked to be reinstated as a teacher. The school was unwilling to make a commitment to him. After the trial was over, however, Scopes was offered his job provided he did not teach evolution. Scopes never did accept the offer. Instead he took money that some of the expert witnesses had set aside for him, attended graduate school in Chicago, and received a

John Scopes taught mathematics, physics, chemistry, and general science in this building during the 1924–1925 school year. Late in the year, he substituted as a biology teacher and used a textbook that he knew contained evolutionary theories.

degree in geology, a field he worked in the rest of his life. He never taught again in the public schools.

The summer of 1925 became one of the hottest summers in legal history. It was a summer John Scopes would never be able to forget. The public would not let him. Thirty years after his death, the name of John Scopes commands great attention as the teacher who challenged the Tennessee monkey law.

chapter five

TWO ATTORNEYS CLASH

COURTHOUSE—Two well-known lawyers attracted the media's interest during the *Scopes* trial. These were no ordinary lawyers. These two men clashed and snarled at each other, adding to the drama and interest in what otherwise might have been a rather dull trial.

The attorney for the prosecution (the state of Tennessee), William Jennings Bryan, served as a special prosecutor, an attorney appointed for a limited and special purpose only. Interested in the issue of evolution, Bryan jumped at the chance to be involved. Once Clarence Darrow learned that Bryan had joined the prosecution, he offered his services without charge to defend John Scopes.

What was it that brought these two well-known attorneys to Dayton, Tennessee, during the summer of 1925?

For the Prosecution: William Jennings Bryan

William Jennings Bryan, known through the entire country for his big booming voice that could fill any auditorium, had run for president of the United States in the 1896, 1900, and 1908 elections. Each election ended in the same way. He lost.

Background

Born in 1860 in Salem, Illinois, the same town where John Scopes had graduated from high school, William Jennings Bryan graduated from Illinois College in Jacksonville. Later he received a law degree from Union College of Law in Chicago. After four years of practicing law in Jacksonville, Illinois, Bryan moved to Lincoln, Nebraska, where he and

Joining the Scopes *trial attorneys for the prosecution was William Jennings Bryan, a three-time candidate for the United States presidency who argued in favor of the Butler Act. Bryan had earlier lobbied for laws prohibiting the teaching of evolution.*

his wife raised three children. One of the children, William Jennings Bryan, Jr., became a lawyer and joined the team of prosecution attorneys at the trial. Once Bryan entered the world of politics, he did not practice law again until the *Scopes* trial, nearly thirty-eight years later.

Public Service

William Jennings Bryan served as a representative from Nebraska in the United States House of Representatives for two terms, 1891–1895. When the Democratic party first nominated him for president in 1896, Bryan was only thirty-six years old, one year older than the minimum required age for a president. Later, during President Woodrow Wilson's term, Bryan served as secretary of state.

Causes He Supported

Bryan became known as the Great Commoner because he supported causes ordinary people identified with. He encouraged the addition of several amendments to the United States Constitution that were later approved. Some of those were the following:

1. The Sixteenth Amendment, which favored an income tax, passed in 1913.

2. The Seventeenth Amendment, which gave the people instead of the state lawmakers the right to elect their senators, passed in 1913.

3. The Nineteenth Amendment, which gave women the right to vote, passed in 1920.

Bryan worked to pass laws that gave compensation to workers who were injured on the job. He favored an eight-hour workday and supported a minimum-wage law. He promoted establishing public parks and wanted international disputes settled by peaceful means.[1] Politically, Bryan was a liberal. He was in favor of social change that was accomplished through government actions. His religion, however, would be described as conservative, resistant to change, favoring traditional ways.

Career

Besides being a political figure, Bryan worked as editor in chief of the *Omaha World Herald*. In 1901, he founded a sixteen-page weekly paper known as *The Commoner*, which ran for twenty-three years and had a circulation of one hundred forty thousand. Bryan, the author of fifteen books, was also known for his speaking ability. His witty remarks and loud, clear voice made him a favorite presenter. His first radio address in 1922 drew a listening audience of 60 million people. Bryan gave as many as twenty-five speeches a day while on the campaign trail. For about thirty years, Bryan accepted some two hundred speaking invitations a year.[2]

In 1925, Bryan lived in Miami, Florida, where he led a weekly Bible class that met in a park and grew to some five thousand people.[3] Considering his popularity as a speaker, it would be no surprise that he was often asked to speak at the graduations in his own hometown of Salem, Illinois, where in 1918 he delivered the address to John Scopes's graduating class. Neither Scopes nor Bryan could have known their paths would cross again seven years later.

Dayton Welcomes Bryan

In the last years of William Jennings Bryan's life, he took on his most fervent cause and campaigned against the teaching of the theories of Darwin on evolution. He supported the right of citizens to decide what would be taught in their schools, and he was convinced that none of them wanted evolution taught to their children. Bryan's beliefs brought him to the trial in hopes of winning a victory for his cause. Considering that most of the people in Dayton, Tennessee, agreed with Bryan, he was welcomed with great enthusiasm.

William Jennings Bryan, a noted public speaker and antievolutionist, preaches to a crowd of some ten thousand people who gathered at the Rhea County Courthouse on Sunday, July 12, 1925. Later in the trial, Bryan stood on this same platform as he was cross-examined as a Bible expert by Scopes's attorney, Clarence Darrow.

However, when Bryan offered to serve as a prosecutor, he prompted a skilled, well-seasoned lawyer by the name of Clarence Darrow to volunteer his services free to John Scopes. Supposedly, Scopes was the only client to whom Darrow did not charge a fee during his legal career.

For the Defense: Clarence Darrow

Just as Bryan had reasons for coming to Dayton, Tennessee, so too did Clarence Darrow. Darrow was known as one of the best defense attorneys in the United States. A defense attorney is the person who represents someone who is being charged with a crime or being sued by another citizen. This attorney seeks to protect the client's rights and oppose the charges against that client—within the guidelines of the law. Darrow was not only interested in law. Other subjects fascinated him too, and one of them was religion. "His Bible was as well thumbed as any preacher ['s Bible] . . . and he gave biblical study as much priority as a preacher."[4] A skilled criminal trial lawyer, Darrow spent most of his career trying unusual and difficult cases. A trial like Scopes's was exactly the kind of case he enjoyed.

Background and Career

Born in 1857 in Kinsman, Ohio, Darrow was the fifth son of a furniture maker. Darrow attended law school at the University of Michigan and began practicing law in Ohio. By 1887, he moved to Chicago to work for the city and eventually became a corporate lawyer for the Chicago and Northwestern Railway.

Trial lawyer Clarence Darrow represented many clients charged with unpopular crimes and agreed to take the John Scopes's case without being paid.

In 1894, Eugene V. Debs, a union representative for the American Railway Union, was arrested for disrupting mail during the Pullman Strike. Darrow chose to leave the comforts of being a corporate lawyer and agreed to be Debs's attorney. Representing Eugene Debs was the beginning of a long and distinguished career as a defense attorney. A remarkable memory and zeal for the causes of the unprivileged drove him.

Causes He Supported

Darrow became interested in the work of unions. He successfully got Debs released from prison. Later in his career, in 1911, Darrow represented the McNamara brothers, who were charged with bombing the Los Angeles Times Building. Although Darrow's efforts spared these brothers from the death penalty, the case cost him the support of the unions and many other clients. "It was not until years later and the case of the boy-killers of Bobbie Franks in 1924 that his reputation was restored."[5]

Leopold and Loeb

At nearly seventy years of age, Darrow took on two of the most challenging cases of his career. Nathan F. Leopold, Jr., and Richard A. Loeb admitted that they had kidnapped and killed a fourteen-year-old boy, Bobbie Franks. Darrow argued that the boys were mentally ill and introduced psychological evidence to prove his case. His defense spared the two their lives, and one of Darrow's causes, opposing the death penalty, had won a major victory.

The *Scopes* Trial

In 1925, at the age of sixty-eight, Darrow agreed to be involved in probably the most famous case of his career—the trial of John T. Scopes. Darrow, an atheist (one who does not believe in God) opposed the work of the fundamentalist movement. He believed education was being threatened by religious fanaticism.[6]

Darrow, as much as Bryan, liked media attention. According to one writer, each lawyer vied for press attention. They

It was standing room only in the hot, second-floor courtroom of the Rhea County Courthouse while lawyers William Jennings Bryan (front left, leaning over table) and Clarence Darrow talk to each other. The empty chairs in the front were for the jurors, who were excused for much of the trial testimony.

took the limelight while the serious-minded schoolteacher was forgotten.[7]

At first the ACLU did not want Darrow to be John Scopes's lawyer. The organization feared the case would turn into a carnival. In the end, John Scopes selected Clarence Darrow to head up his defense team.[8]

Although the ACLU may not have wanted Darrow or the carnival-like publicity the trial drew, almost overnight, this new organization became well known.

Dayton Welcomes Darrow

In an attempt to be impartial, the Dayton Progressive Club that welcomed Bryan also honored Darrow at a dinner. Darrow attempted to win the favor of the townspeople, but was unable to do so.[9] He was given the title of Colonel. Bryan had announced the trial would be a "duel to the death." Darrow responded, "We will smother Mr. Bryan's influence under a mountain of scientific testimony."[10]

Later Darrow commented that the people of Dayton, Tennessee, were nice to him, even though his beliefs differed from theirs. The two attorneys, Bryan and Darrow, did not have much time for each other either inside the courtroom or outside. Darrow wrote later about the trial, "No one ever displayed the least sign of discourtesy, except perhaps Mr. and Mrs. Bryan . . . they glanced the other way any time we were at all near each other."[11]

When Raulston ruled against the defense motion to set aside the indictment (charge) against Scopes, Darrow was not surprised, but he was bitter.[12] Darrow, it might be said, failed to take into consideration the judge in this case—a man from a mountain town raised by a Christian woman who read the Bible to him every night. This judge was not about to change his views because Clarence Darrow was in his courtroom. Fifteen years after the trial, John Raulston spoke about his views and confirmed why he could not disavow the antievolution law any more than Darrow could approve it.

> The people of Tennessee are profoundly fundamental in their religious beliefs . . . they attribute their existence to the divine Creation. . . . The Tennessee legislature passed the act, the governor had signed it, a federal judge in Knoxville

William Jennings Bryan (left) and the prosecution in the Scopes *trial argued that John Scopes violated Tennessee law by teaching evolution. Clarence Darrow (right) was the lawyer who defended John T. Scopes. That case led to further debate about the issue of evolution being taught in public schools.*

had refused to issue an injunction against it. Now could he [Darrow] have expected a small town trial judge of the criminal court, who agreed wholeheartedly with the law, to set the law aside?"[13]

In an unusual trial strategy, Darrow called William Jennings Bryan to the witness stand near the end of the trial. Bryan agreed, and Judge Raulston, seeing that Bryan did not object, allowed the testimony, although the next day the testimony was "struck from" (taken out of) the court record.

Darrow's examination (questioning) of Bryan became one of the best-known parts of the trial. Darrow had been waiting for the chance to challenge Bryan. Two years earlier, Darrow had written fifty-five questions about the Bible for Bryan to answer. Those questions, published on the front page of the July 4, 1923, *Chicago Tribune*, became the basis for Darrow's cross-examination. Bryan had ignored them when they were originally published. This time he could not.[14]

So it was that Bryan and Darrow met in Dayton, taking on a controversial battle. The far-reaching effect of the trial would ripple down to the present day. Each summer in July, Dayton, Tennessee, rolls back time to 1925 and reenacts the trial of the century.

chapter six

JUDGE AND JURY

COURTHOUSE—There were not many big trials held in Judge John Raulston's circuit. Judge Raulston probably knew the *Scopes* trial would be an opportunity for him, and when he received the chance to try the case, he did not hesitate. In fact, Raulston had big expectations for this trial. He even suggested that a roof be built over a large vacant lot so twenty thousand people could be seated in tiers to hear the trial.[1]

Grand Jury

Judge Raulston's first responsibility, however, was to call a special grand jury, and he did. This jury met on May 25, 1925, in Dayton. They issued an indictment (charge of a crime) against John Scopes. Since local businesspeople had feared that Chattanooga or some other Tennessee city might snatch the trial out of their hands, Judge Raulston quickly scheduled a time for the grand jury to meet.

Later, however, legal questions were raised over the grand jury. To correct any legal errors, Judge Raulston again called the grand jury at the beginning of the court trial on July 10. Again he read them the Butler Act and the Creation story from Genesis. He instructed them to investigate the alleged offense without prejudice or bias and with open minds. If a violation was found, they should return an indictment.[2]

The grand jury met in secret to decide whether to indict John Scopes. Three of Scopes's students were called to tell the grand jury that Scopes had taught evolution, but they feared they would get their teacher in trouble and ran away. John Scopes himself had to find them and persuade them to testify.[3] At 11:00 A.M. the grand jury reappeared and gave Judge Raulston a bill of indictment. For the second time, the grand jury had reached the same decision. The trial known as *State of Tennessee* v. *John Thomas Scopes* was now ready for trial.

Trial Jury Selection

After Scopes's indictment, the selection of a trial jury became the first order of business. Clarence Darrow, the defense attorney, soon learned that Tennessee did not maintain a regular jury list for lesser cases. Sixteen potential jurors were in court. It seemed the jurors would be selected from bystanders if more jurors were needed.[4]

The Tennessee jury selection process no doubt frustrated Clarence Darrow. Each side had three preemptory challenges, or the right to remove three jurors from the panel for any cause. In his experience, Darrow was used to selecting his jury *after* he had questioned all the potential jurors. In Tennessee, however, a preemptory challenge had to be exercised immediately after a potential juror was questioned. In addition to the preemptory challenges, a juror could be struck "for cause," such as not being able to make a fair decision or knowing one of the parties or attorneys. A minister was struck for cause.

Darrow asked each juror three questions:

1. Do you know anything about evolution?

2. Do you have an opinion whether or not the Bible is against evolution?

3. Would you make up your mind based on the evidence presented in the case?[5]

Twelve men were selected to serve as jurors. Eight were dismissed for various reasons. One of the jurors admitted he could not read, and several others said they had read only from the Bible. Eleven of the twelve were church members, and all but one were farmers or owned farms.[6]

Clarence Darrow said of the jury, "It is as we expected." A July 11, 1925, Memphis paper read, "No Modernists Named on the Scopes Jury; all Believe in Bible."[7] Judge Raulston announced, with the jury selection complete, that court would reconvene on Monday, July 13. Who was this judge who presided over the *Scopes* trial?

Judge John Raulston

Judge John Raulston, born in Gizzards Cove, had lived in Tennessee his whole life. He thought of himself as ordinary, and even described himself as "just a regular mountain judge."[8] Regardless, Judge Raulston also enjoyed publicity, and it was not unlike him to recess the court proceedings for a "photo shoot." On the first day of the trial, Raulston delayed opening court so the radio engineers could connect their microphones and set them up in the courtroom. He proudly announced, "My gavel will be heard around the world."[9]

Raulston, who followed the fundamentalist movement, carried his Bible with his law books. Over the defense attorneys' objections, Raulston insisted on opening each day of court with prayer, a practice that was unfamiliar to the defense attorneys. Darrow objected to all prayer, and although Raulston continued to open each day with an invocation, the defense's continual objections must have finally worn on Judge Raulston. When the trial was moved outdoors, Raulston did grant Darrow's request to remove a banner from the courthouse that read, "Read Your Bible."

Judge Raulston served as a judge of a Tennessee circuit court that included seven counties; Rhea County, where Dayton was located, being one of them. He traveled between several courthouses in his circuit and held trials as the need arose.

When Judge Raulston stepped up to the bench in Dayton, he could not leave his beliefs behind. He favored the prosecution.[10] In a speech he gave in New York City after the trial, Raulston expressed his viewpoint, "If I lose faith in Genesis, I'm afraid I'll lose faith in the rest of the Bible."[11]

Although Raulston wanted to be the judge, he seemed unsure of himself at times. He frequently excused the jury from the court proceedings so that witnesses would not influence them. Ironically, apparently the jurors heard some of the forbidden testimony anyway. One account said, "Reporters looked out the window and saw the jurors sitting in the courthouse yard listening to the arguments over the loudspeakers."[12]

Judge Raulston also took considerable time in making a decision on the defense motion to set aside the indictment against Scopes. He became overly alarmed when he thought someone had leaked the decision to the newspapers. He called an investigation of the matter only to discover that he himself had slipped and told a reporter.[13] He also kept putting off making a decision about whether the defense expert witnesses would be allowed to testify. Instead he forced them to wait. Raulston appeared to be in no hurry to rush what might be Dayton's finest moment. It was not until Wednesday, July 15, in the afternoon, that the first witness was called to testify. Three-and-one-half days had been spent selecting a jury and arguing over the validity of Tennessee's Butler Act. The media became restless and many of the onlookers went home.

Judge Raulston was concerned about more than just technical legal matters. The heat and the stability of the courthouse floor also absorbed his attention. Because the trial was located on the second floor of the courthouse, Raulston feared that the room, which would normally seat about four hundred people, could not bear the weight of the nearly one thousand people in it. On the seventh day of the trial, after inspecting cracks in the first-floor ceiling, he moved the proceedings outdoors. The *Scopes* trial became known as the "trial on the lawn."

The suffocating heat in the courtroom rose to over 100 degrees. Jurors waved fans, and a small electric fan cooled Judge Raulston. Judge Raulston authorized the attorneys and court personnel to dispense with the courtroom dress requirement and allowed them to remove coats and ties.[14]

Many of the people waved palm leaves, common in the days before air-conditioning. Even electric fans were rare. When a juror said, "If it ain't out of order, I would like to make the request, the unanimous request of the jury to take up the matter of some electric fans here. This heat is fearful," he was told that on account of the depleted state of the county treasury they could not afford the fans. Attorney for the defense, Malone, piped up, "I will buy some fans."[15]

The sleeves of attorney Bryan's shirt were rolled up as high as they could go. Behind him, his wife, Mary, watched from a wheelchair. She suffered not only from the heat but also from crippling arthritis. It was reported that she privately objected to her husband's involvement in the trial, but she endured the heat and the trial in "quiet dignity."[16]

As much as Judge Raulston tried to secure the loyalty of the public, he must have failed. He lost his bid for reelection in 1926.

A Long Trial

The *Scopes* trial spanned ten days, from July 10, 1925, to noon on Tuesday, July 21. Boring legal matters took up the first three days of the trial. On the fourth day of the trial,

Wednesday, July 15, Scopes finally entered his plea, "Not guilty," and the prosecution was ready to present their case and witnesses to the jury. The balance of the trial would be dominated by the defense, but to little avail. All of the testimony of their witnesses would eventually be excluded, and even though Judge Raulston would allow attorney Bryan to be questioned, even his statements would be struck from the court record.

The Issues of the Trial

Many questions arose as a result of the *Scopes* trial. The question for the prosecution remained a simple one: Did John Scopes violate the Butler Act by teaching a "theory that denies the story of the Divine Creation of man as taught in the Bible, and to teach instead that man has descended from a lower order of animals?"

The main question for the defense remained whether the Butler Act violated the First Amendment of the Constitution of the United States. They contended that such a law

Scopes *trial judge John T. Raulston, of Tennessee Circuit Court, decided to set the fine for John Scopes instead of letting the jury impose it. This action allowed the Tennessee Supreme Court to dismiss the charges against Scopes. The case could not be appealed as the defense had hoped.*

violated freedom of speech and the prohibition on establishment of religion.

These questions were not the only ones at stake in a trial like this. Other issues were the following:

1. Modernism versus fundamentalism

2. Evolution versus Creation

3. Separation of church and state

4. Governmental authority versus taxpayers' rights

5. Free speech versus censorship

6. Academic freedom of teachers versus academic freedom of students and student rights[17]

Religious beliefs clashed with new scientific theories of the day. That collision made the *Scopes* trial the sort of thing that grabs headlines and makes for a notable trial. It was no surprise that thousands gathered in Dayton to hear what would happen.

chapter seven

THE CASE FOR TENNESSEE

STATE'S CASE—After John Scopes entered a "not guilty" plea to the charges against him, A. Thomas Stewart, the chief prosecutor and attorney general for the state of Tennessee, stood to address the court. His opening statement took less than a minute.

"It is the insistence of the state in this case that the defendant, John Thomas Scopes, has violated the antievolution law, by teaching in the public schools of Rhea county the theory tending to show that man and mankind is descended from a lower order of animals."[1]

The prosecution did not view the case as being complex. Instead its case centered on whether a law had been broken and whether the defendant was guilty of breaking that law. Stewart, for the state of Tennessee, sought to prove that John Scopes taught evolution in the Rhea County High School in Dayton and had violated the law. Stewart would ask the jury to find Scopes guilty and impose a fine for this misdemeanor violation.

Stewart, who headed the prosecution, presented himself as a no-nonsense type of lawyer. He seemed to be a voice of reason later in the trial when tempers flared between William Jennings Bryan and Clarence Darrow. At one point on the seventh day of the trial, Stewart pleaded with Judge Raulston to stop the exchange between Bryan and Darrow and restore order. Raulston did not stop the questions between the two, but Stewart's attempts left an impression. H. L. Mencken, a famous newspaper reporter at the trial, described Stewart as "a man of apparent education and sense." After the trial, Stewart won election as a United States senator for Tennessee.[2]

John Scopes, with his hands clasped behind his back, stands in the center of a crowd gathered at the start of his trial.

Other attorneys joined the prosecutors. Several played minor roles in the entire courtroom drama, such as two Dayton lawyers who were brothers, Sue (named for his mother) and Herbert Hicks. William Jennings Bryan, Jr., spoke very little. Unlike his father, who possessed one of the finest speaking voices, he spoke so softly during the trial that on two occasions he was asked to speak louder.[3]

The assistant attorney general, Ben G. McKenzie, became known for his playful gestures. He liked calling defense attorney Clarence Darrow the Colonel. He also mentioned that the meeting with Darrow was "love at first sight." Even though he may have appeared to be pleasant and humorous, Ben McKenzie took jabs at the big-city lawyers from New York and Chicago. Once he suggested that they "go back home and teach their thugs, thieves and rioters." He thought they should quit trying to change the people in the South who believed Genesis told the full story of Creation.[4]

Ironically, as bold and as outspoken as William Jennings Bryan was about evolution, the great commoner did not speak in the trial until the defense presented its case to the court. It was at that time that William Jennings Bryan stated his views about the case and the admissibility of the defense expert witnesses. Bryan began,

> If the court please we are now approaching the end of the first week of this trial and I haven't thought it proper until this time to take part in the discussions. . . . I have been tempted to speak at former times, but I have been able to withstand the temptation.[5]

Bryan continued in his support of the Butler Act:

> In the first place, the statute—our position is that the statute is sufficient. The statute defines exactly what the people of Tennessee desired and intended and did declare unlawful and it needs no interpretation.[6]

Bryan was a firm believer that taxpayers had the right to determine what course of study would be taught in the schools. He had this to say: "This is not the place to try to prove that the law ought never to have been passed. The

William Jennings Bryan addresses the court as an attorney for the prosecution. Ben McKenzie, sits listening next to him. Chicago radio station WGN, still in existence today, placed microphones in the courtroom, establishing the Scopes *trial as the first American trial to be broadcast.*

place to prove that, or teach that, was to the [lawmakers]."[7] Although Bryan may have thought the case should have a narrow focus and remain on the law, he forgot his own advice and in the heat of the trial broadened the issue to his own reading and interpretation of the Bible. Excerpts from his testimony are included in the next chapter.

The prosecution, in essence, argued "that the state, through the legislature, had the right to control its schools by prescribing the content of their curriculum."[8]

After the prosecution's opening statement, the defense attorneys made a motion to dismiss the case against Scopes, which Judge Raulston denied. Even though they knew Raulston would not grant their request, the defense attorneys made the motion anyway. This legal move would give an appellate court grounds to overturn the lower court's decision.

Prosecution Calls Witnesses

The state of Tennessee called four witnesses to testify.

Superintendent of Schools, Walter White. The first witness, Walter White, the superintendent of schools, said that he had been at Rhea County Central High School for six-and-one-half years. He testified that Mr. Scopes admitted teaching evolution in the classroom in these words, "Scopes told me that he had reviewed the entire book [Hunter's *A Civic Biology*] during certain days in April . . . and among other things he said he could not teach that book without teaching evolution." White went on to say that Scopes defended his right to teach evolution and thought the Butler Act was unconstitutional.[9]

Although it did not seem relevant to White's testimony, the prosecutors introduced a copy of the King James Version of the Bible while he was on the witness stand. Prosecutor Stewart told the court that they were offering the Bible as evidence to explain what the Butler Act meant when it said, "Bible." The defense objected, and Judge Raulston overruled their objection. The Bible was marked as an exhibit. Hunter's *A Civic Biology* had already been received as a part of the trial exhibits.[10]

Clarence Darrow asked to get a copy of the Bible that the prosecution had introduced. Judge Raulston indicated that he could probably obtain a copy of it at Robinson's Drugstore, but Darrow sarcastically responded, "In this small town, I don't know."[11]

White explained that the school had no objection to Scopes's work as a teacher. He also explained that the Tennessee Textbook Commission had approved Hunter's *A Civic Biology* as the official text in Tennessee for five years, but the contract had expired on August 31, 1924.[12]

Student, Howard Morgan. The next witness for the state was a fourteen-year-old student of Scopes's. Howard Morgan's father was a banker at the Dayton Bank and Trust, and Clarence Darrow and his wife were guests at their home during the trial. Although Howard Morgan was a witness for the state of Tennessee, Clarence Darrow, the defense attorney, prepared him for his testimony on the witness stand.

Howard Morgan talked about what Scopes had taught in

the biology class. The boy was asked to state in his own words what Scopes had said. Howard Morgan gave his prepared response in one long sentence:

> He said that the earth was once a hot molten mass, too hot for plant or animal life to exist upon it; in the sea the earth cooled off; there was a little germ of one cell organism formed, and this organism kept evolving until it got to be a pretty good-sized animal, and then came on to be a land animal, and it kept on evolving, and from this was man.[13]

After Stewart finished his questions, Clarence Darrow cross-examined Howard Morgan and asked whether he remembered what made an animal a mammal. When Morgan did not seem to recall, Darrow asked whether

Four attorneys for the prosecution gather in the crowded courtroom to discuss strategy. Second from left to right: Attorney General A. T. Stewart, William Jennings Bryan, Jr. (son of William Jennings Bryan), William Jennings Bryan, and Sue K. Hicks (Dayton attorney).

Scopes had told him that dogs, horses, monkeys, cows, man, and whales were all mammals. The student agreed, but then admitted he did not know if whales were mammals. There was laughter in the courtroom. After the courtroom quieted, Darrow asked, "Well, did he tell you anything else that was wicked?" The youth answered, "No, not that I remember of."[14]

Student, Harry Shelton. Harry Shelton, a seventeen-year-old student at Dayton's high school, was called to testify. He said John Scopes had taught him for about three weeks in April 1925, and part of that instruction included evolution. Shelton said Scopes had reviewed Hunter's *A Civic Biology* textbook with the class and taught them that all forms of life begin with the cell. On cross-examination, Darrow asked if Shelton was a church member. Shelton answered, "Yes, sir." Then Darrow asked, "You didn't leave church when he told you all forms of life began with a single cell?" Shelton said, "No, sir." Darrow then concluded his cross-examination with, "That is all."[15]

Chairman of the School Board, F. E. Robinson. The last witness for the state of Tennessee was F. E. Robinson, an original promoter of the trial and the owner of Robinson's Drugstore, where school textbooks were sold. Robinson also served as chairman of the Rhea County School Board. When asked whether he and Scopes had spoken about the teaching of evolution, Robinson said that Scopes told him, "Any teacher in the State who was teaching Hunter's Biology was violating the law; [and] that science teachers could not teach Hunter's Biology without violating the law."[16]

Darrow, on cross-examination, held up a copy of *A Civic Biology* and asked Robinson: "You were selling them, were you not?" Robinson responded, "Yes, sir." Laughter broke out in the courtroom. Then Darrow said with his wry humor, "I think someone ought to advise you that you are not bound to answer these questions." Unimpressed with Darrow's humor, prosecutor Thomas Stewart spoke in Robinson's defense, "The law says teach, not sell."[17]

Robinson admitted he had sold the textbook for six or seven years. Then Darrow asked him, "Have you noticed any mental or moral deterioration growing out of the thing?" Before Robinson could answer, the prosecution objected to Darrow's question and Judge Raulston sustained the objection, which meant that Robinson did not have to respond.[18]

The prosecuting attorneys asked for an opportunity to read the first two chapters of Genesis from the Bible into the court record. To their surprise, Darrow even responded, "No objection to that."[19]

Although the state had five other witnesses ready, because the testimony would have been similar to what others had said, the state chose to rest. Their case began at 1:00 P.M. on the fourth day of the trial, July 15, 1925, and finished at 4:00 P.M. that same day. The audience now looked to the defense to present its case.

chapter eight

THE CASE FOR JOHN SCOPES

COURTROOM—The *Scopes* trial was more than a legal tool, at least for the defense team of lawyers and the ACLU. They wanted an opportunity to educate the public about the science of evolution. The defense hoped to prove that evolution was an accepted scientific theory, and that any law that did not allow this theory to be taught in the schools violated First Amendment freedoms, one of which was freedom of speech.

Freedom of speech does not guarantee a right to say whatever a person wants to. For example, a person would not be protected for shouting, "Fire!" in a theater and creating a panic when there was no fire. Other restrictions on freedom of speech include certain types of obscenity, defaming another person's reputation with false accusations, and using fighting words that might provoke a riot. Another area that is not protected is hate speech, which is speech designed to hurt people based on their race or religion.

Schools can also restrict

speech that would disrupt their educational purposes. Yet students may use symbolic speech to express views. Mary Beth and John Tinker wore black armbands to school in the 1960s to protest the Vietnam War. The school suspended them. The Supreme Court in 1969, however, ruled that teachers and students do not "shed their constitutional rights to freedom of speech or expression at the schoolhouse gate."[1] In other words, freedom of speech is also granted to students and teachers in schools.

The defense team of attorneys in *Scopes* was prepared to argue that a teacher had a right, if not a duty, to educate students about certain well-known and accepted theories even if the students might not agree with the theory. For this team of lawyers, freedom of speech guaranteed the right to teach evolution in the classroom.

After the prosecution finished with its case, the defense attorneys began what they hoped would be their finest moments.

The personalities of the attorneys contributed to the mood that was described as a "trial set for a duel to the death between science and revealed religion."[2] Besides Clarence Darrow, the best-known attorneys for the defense were Dudley Field Malone, Arthur Garfield Hays, and John Randolph Neal.

Dudley Field Malone. A New York lawyer and a superb speaker, Malone received the loudest applause during the trial when he argued why the expert testimony should be allowed in the trial. He became known as the attorney who, despite the sweltering heat, never removed his suit coat.

Arthur Garfield Hays. This New York attorney who represented the ACLU was assigned the technical parts of the trial. It was his role to guarantee that the case could be appealed to a higher court. For this reason, the attorneys for Scopes made many "objections" during the trial, even though many were overruled by the judge. If an appellate court believed some of those decisions by the judge were in error, a decision could be reversed (changed). Hays commented about the trial, "The people of the country learned more about evolution through the Dayton exhibition than they could have in any other way."[3]

John Randolph Neal. John Scopes's first attorney on the

International divorce lawyer Dudley Field Malone worked closely with Clarence Darrow on the defense of John Scopes. Malone's response to Bryan's arguments drew applause from the audience.

case offered his services to the young teacher. A law school professor, Neal had lost his position with the University of Tennessee because of his opinions on evolution. He saw the case as a fight for civil liberty (the right to speak) more than a case about religious and scientific differences.[4]

Dudley Field Malone gave the opening statement for the defense. Unlike the short opening statement of Thomas Stewart, Malone gave a lengthy explanation of what the defense would do in the trial. He claimed the defense would do the following:

1. It would prove that science and religion occupy two different fields of learning.

2. It would prove that scientists claim that no branch of science can be taught without teaching evolution.

3. It *did not* intend to prove that humans came from the monkey.[5]

Malone also argued that the defense intended to help form intelligent opinions about the value of teaching the theory of evolution. He claimed the narrow purpose of the defense was to establish the innocence of Scopes. The broad purpose was to prove the Bible as a work of religious inspiration that must be kept in the field of theology and not science.[6]

Although the defense had no intention of calling Scopes as a witness, they did want their expert witnesses to have an opportunity to explain evolution. They also wanted several religious leaders to testify that evolution and the Creation account in the Bible did not oppose each other, a view

decide whether the expert witnesses would be allowed to testify. The defense attorneys did not want to waste their time. Judge Raulston refused to decide that issue at the beginning of the trial. Now he was presented with the same question again except that by now, many of the experts had been in Dayton for nearly a week.

Would those experts be allowed to testify? The prosecution objected to any expert testimony and claimed it was not important to the case. Judge Raulston, hesitant to make a final decision, decided to allow the testimony of one expert witness and reserved the right to decide later whether to include the testimony. The jury was excused, and Clarence Darrow called Maynard M. Metcalf to the witness stand. Metcalf admitted he was an evolutionist. He also said he was a member of the Congregational Church and taught a Bible class at his church.[17]

Darrow asked Metcalf, "Do you know any scientific man in the world that is not an evolutionist?" Before Metcalf had an opportunity to respond, the prosecutors objected to the question. The court sustained the objection, which meant that Metcalf was not allowed to give an answer. In a clever maneuver, Darrow then asked the court to include in the court record what Mr. Metcalf would have said had he been allowed to speak. Metcalf responded,

> I am acquainted with practically all of the zoologists, botanists and geologists of this country who have done any work . . . and I am absolutely convinced from personal knowledge that any one of these men feel and believe, as a matter of course, that evolution is a fact."[18]

Metcalf also gave the following definition for evolution: "The change of an organism from one character into a different character, and by character I mean its structure, or its behavior, or its function, or its method of development. . . ."[19]

Judge Raulston, concerned that the jury might read Metcalf's testimony in the paper, instructed reporters not to have any of the testimony printed.[20] He also grew impatient with Darrow's questions, and asked, "Col. Darrow, will this extend very much further? It has been a pretty hard day for me." Darrow promised to only ask three or four more questions.[21]

Court adjourned for the day. The next morning, on Thursday, July 16, Darrow fully expected to continue to question Metcalf. Instead the debate over the admissibility of the testimony of the defense expert witnesses continued. Defense attorney Hays argued that expert testimony must be included for the defense to properly present its case. He had told a story about a judge who once turned to a defendant and said, "I don't care to hear anything from the defendant, to hear both sides has a tendency to confuse the court." Laughter broke out in the courtroom.[22]

Then William Jennings Bryan rose to speak for the first time in the trial. He argued the validity of the statute. He also argued that no expert testimony should be allowed. But he did not stick to that topic. Instead, he looked at Hunter's *A Civic Biology* and turned to page 194. Pointing to the textbook, Bryan read, "Man descended from Old World monkeys."[23] In his biting response he added that he supposed "that each child is expected to copy the family tree and take it home to his family to be submitted for the Bible family tree." Again Bryan was unable to limit his remarks and began a personal attack on Darrow for his involvement in the Leopold and Loeb case in Chicago where Darrow had represented two young men accused of murder and had spared them the death penalty. Bryan urged the court to cut off expert witnesses and finish up the case.[24]

Then Dudley Malone responded to Bryan. His remarks were pointed.

> . . . let the children have their minds kept open–close no door to their knowledge; shut no door from them. Make the distinction between theology and science. Let them have both. . . . We are ready to tell the truth as we understand it. We feel we stand with progress. We feel we stand with science. We feel we stand with intelligence . . . we ask your honor to admit the evidence as a matter of correct law.[25]

There was profound and continued applause for Malone's statement. The clash between the lawyers became so intense that Judge Raulston warned that there should be no display of emotions in the courtroom and especially no applause. He said that it was improper and he feared that the heavily weighted floor might give out.[26]

After extensive argument from both sides on whether the experts should be allowed to testify, Judge Raulston adjourned court. The next day, he announced his decision to grant the motion of the prosecution to exclude the expert testimony. Instead of witnesses giving testimony in court, they would be allowed to read their opinions into the court record or submit them in writing. The jury never would hear what they had to say. The defense lawyers were given the weekend to get their documents ready, statements that would contain nearly thirty-five thousand words.[27] An appellate court (higher court) could then determine if Judge Raulston's ruling was correct in excluding them as witnesses.

Darrow, upset by the ruling to exclude expert witness testimony, spouted his anger at Judge Raulston: "I do not understand why every request of the state and every suggestion of the prosecution should meet with an endless waste of time, and a bare suggestion of anything that is perfectly competent on our part should be immediately overruled." Raulston asked, "I hope you do not mean to reflect upon the court?" Darrow responded, "Well, your honor has the right to hope."[28] The court adjourned for the weekend.

Judge Raulston must have thought about Darrow's crisp comments, and wondered if he should find him in contempt. If he did so, Darrow would be penalized for having violated the courtroom proceedings or judges orders.

Thinking the trial was all but over, many of the media packed their bags and left. WGN from Chicago and H. L. Mencken for the *Baltimore Sun* pulled out of town for more interesting assignments. Several of the attorneys left for home, including William Jennings Bryan, Jr. The pending contempt charge on Darrow was not enough to hold their attention. What they did not realize was they would miss the best and most remembered part of the trial—Darrow's cross-examination of Bryan.

Contempt Charge Cited

When court reconvened on Monday morning, July 20, after an opening prayer, Judge Raulston announced that Darrow was in contempt of court for his comments. The judge set bail at five thousand dollars. Later that day, Darrow apologized to the judge and explained that he had been a lawyer for forty-seven years and had been very busy taking cases where he had to fight public opinion—even in his hometown of Chicago. He admitted that he had in this case gone further than he should have and "one thing snapped out after another."[29]

Raulston forgave Darrow the contempt charge, but used the occasion to express his religious beliefs: "The Man that I believe came into the world to save man from sin . . . taught that it was godly to forgive. . . . I believe in that Christ. I believe in these principles. I accept Colonel Darrow's apology."[30]

From the Courtroom to the Courtyard

Fearing the floor might collapse, Judge Raulston moved the court proceedings from the courtroom to the outdoor courtyard. Outside, Darrow noticed the large sign that hung from the courthouse wall, "READ YOUR BIBLE," and asked Judge Raulston to remove it. Judge Raulston may have surprised everyone when he granted the request and said, "If the presence of the sign irritates anyone, or if anyone thinks it might influence the jury in any way, I have no purpose except to give both sides a fair trial in this case. Feeling that way about it, I will let the sign come down."[31]

Cross-Examination of William Jennings Bryan

The defense had no more witnesses of its own. Instead, William Jennings Bryan was asked to testify. His testimony became one of the most fascinating and compelling scenes of the whole trial. Although his own fellow attorneys objected to this highly unusual move to call one of their attorneys to the witness stand, Bryan did not refuse, and the judge allowed him to testify.

On the same platform where he had preached only eight days before, Bryan settled down in the witness chair as an

The trial was moved outside the courthouse on the seventh day of the trial, July 20, 1925, as the defense called William Jennings Bryan to the witness stand. Clarence Darrow (right) cross examines Bryan during what has become one of the best known and most sensational parts of the trial.

expert on the Bible. Again, Judge Raulston asked the jury to leave.

Darrow cross-examined Bryan on many subjects in the Bible, ranging from the flood to Jonah and the whale, to the story of Creation in Genesis. Darrow questioned Bryan about the first chapter of Genesis, and about the time involved in creating the earth.

Q. Mr. Bryan, have you any idea how old the earth is?

A. No.

Q. Do you think the earth was made in six days?

A. Not six days of twenty-four hours.

Q. Doesn't it say so?

A. No, sir.[32]

Fundamentalists gasped at Bryan's response and then sat in silence. To this group, when the Bible said a day they believed that that meant twenty-four hours and to be unsure or to define it as a period of time seemed to support the case for evolution.[33]

Prosecutor Thomas Stewart feared his own witness would soon be at odds with the fundamentalist movement. He objected to the questions and inquired about their purpose. A pale and trembling Bryan rose from the witness stand, shook his fist above his head and shouted, "The purpose is to cast ridicule on everybody who believes in the Bible, and I am willing that the world shall know that these gentlemen have no other purpose than ridiculing every person who believes in the Bible."[34]

Darrow snapped back, "We have the purpose of preventing bigots and ignoramuses from controlling the education of the United States and you know it, and that is all."[35]

Stewart's objections went unnoticed and the debate between Darrow and Bryan intensified.

Judge John Raulston (left) cited Clarence Darrow (right) for contempt of court on July 20, 1925. The judge dismissed the charge after Darrow later apologized, and the men shook hands.

Bryan's response continued: "I am simply trying to protect the word of God against the greatest atheist or agnostic in the United States."[36] Applause broke out in the courtyard. Again prosecutor Thomas Stewart attempted to bring the matter under control. "I call on your honor, in the name of all that is legal, to stop this examination and stop it here."[37]

Again Stewart's appeal to the judge was unsuccessful. The two attorneys continued to argue with each other. Bryan insisted he believed the Bible as it was written, and said, "The only purpose Mr. Darrow has is to slur at the Bible," to which Darrow lashed back, "I object to your statement. I am exempting you on your fool ideas that no intelligent Christian on Earth believes."[38]

Judge Raulston ended the court proceedings abruptly. The battle of the courtyard was over, but the reactions to it would continue for years. After Bryan's testimony, the defense rested (concluded) its case, and later Judge Raulston expunged (removed) Bryan's testimony from the record. Now the case was left to the fate of twelve men. Would they find John Scopes guilty of teaching evolution?

chapter nine

THE JURY DECIDES

On the final day of the *Scopes* trial, Judge Raulston opened court with prayer as he had on all the previous days. This day in court, however, would be different. Darrow, conceding the point that none of his experts would be allowed to testify, said, "Mr. Scopes did teach what the children said he taught, that man descended from a lower order of animals. . . . I think to save time we will ask the court to bring in the jury and instruct the jury to find the defendant guilty."[1]

Judge Raulston gave the jury instructions intended to help them in making a decision. He began:

Gentlemen of the Jury: This is the case of the *State of Tennessee* vs. *John Thomas Scopes*, where it is charged that the accused violated what is commonly known as the antievolution statute . . . to this charge the defendant has pleaded not guilty and thus are made up the issues for your determination. Before there can be a conviction the state must make out its case beyond a reasonable doubt. . . . By the phrase 'beyond a reasonable doubt,' I do not mean any possible doubt . . . [but] such a doubt as would prevent your mind resting easy as to the guilt of the defendant. . . . But if the proof fails to show him guilty beyond a reasonable doubt, you should acquit the defendant and your verdict should be not guilty . . . but you should search for and find the truth, and the truth alone, and bring into this court such a verdict you think truth dictates and justice demands.[2]

Before dismissing the jury, Judge Raulston explained that if they found the defendant guilty and wanted to impose

The twelve jurors listen intently to Judge Raulston's instructions at the end of the trial. These men who sat in front of the room actually heard little of the trial because the judge decided not to let the jury be present for most of the eight-day trial.

a fine of greater than one hundred dollars, they would have to set the fine. But if they wanted no more than a one hundred dollar fine they could leave this decision up to the judge. Prosecuting attorney Thomas Stewart responded that he thought the jury should fix whatever fine was imposed. Judge Raulston assured him that the judge could set a minimum fine.[3] The defense made no objection. None of the attorneys or the judge could have realized that this technicality (whether the jury or the judge would set the fine) would eventually prompt the Tennessee Supreme Court to declare the decision null and void (without effect).

After giving his instructions, Judge Raulston dismissed the jury. At 11:23 A.M., after only nine minutes of deliberation, the twelve men returned to the courtroom. The foreman announced their decision, "We have found for the state, found the defendant guilty."[4] The jury chose not to impose the fine and instead, left that up to the judge's discretion.

Before his sentencing, the defendant spoke in his defense for the first time.

> Your honor, I feel that I have been convicted of violating an unjust statute. I will continue in the future, as I have in the past, to oppose this law in any way I can. Any other action would be in violation of my ideal of academic freedom— that is, to teach the truth as guaranteed in our constitution, of personal and religious freedom. I think the fine is unjust.[5]

Nevertheless, the judge imposed a fine of one hundred dollars and bail was set at five hundred dollars. The bail bond was paid by the *Baltimore Evening Sun* newspaper.

The Appeal to the Tennessee Supreme Court

The excitement of the trial was gone. The defense attorneys responsible for appealing the case failed to communicate. They failed to meet certain deadlines for filing papers, and the American Civil Liberties Union argued over Clarence Darrow's involvement in the case. Even church denominations that did not oppose the teaching of evolution in the schools did not want the controversial Darrow involved in the appeal process.[6] By this time John Scopes was no longer teaching in Tennessee.

On appeal, the defense wanted the Tennessee Supreme Court to declare the Butler Act unconstitutional. The prosecution (called "respondents" on appeal) defended the right of the state of Tennessee to control what could be taught in the public schools.

The Tennessee Supreme Court decided the matter on an unusual point of law. This court reversed the case on the grounds that only a jury could impose a fine of more than fifty dollars. The court also gave its opinion about retrying the case. It pleaded with attorneys to end the matter.

This Court is informed that the plaintiff in error is no longer in the service of the state. We see nothing to be gained by prolonging the life of this bizarre case. On the contrary, we think the peace and dignity of the state . . . will be the better conserved by the entry of a *nolle prosequi* herein. Such a course is suggested to the Attorney General.[7] [*Nolle prosequi* means to prosecute no further. The *Scopes* case was never tried again.]

For forty-two years the Butler Act remained on the

books as "law" in Tennessee—forbidding the teaching of evolution in the classrooms. The case never got to the United States Supreme Court.

The Reaction of the Media

The media (newspapers, magazines, radio) made this trial a sensation, and the reactions to the events of that eight-day trial were numerous.

Some reacted to the end of the trial. *The Dayton Herald* described the end in these words: "The curtain dropped Tuesday noon on the world-watched, nation-wide drama entitled, *The State of Tennessee* vs. *John Thomas Scopes*, when the jury brought in a verdict of guilty . . . a relaxed finish to the bitterest legal battle ever waged in the United States."[8] Another report declared the end a great relief:

> The conclusion of the Scopes trial in Tennessee, one of the strangest in the history of American jurisprudence, is a great relief. . . . The one light in the sky now is the promise of a rest, even if temporary, so that the minds of the people and the columns of the newspapers, may turn to more constructive things.[9]

Another description of Dayton after the trial said: "Dayton's days in the limelight are over, and the town may now relapse into its accustomed obscurity. . . . The jury, of course, have found Mr. Scopes guilty. On the issue put to them by the judge they could do no other."[10] Even religious magazines were relieved to see the end, saying,

> It was fortunate that the so-called trial lasted no longer than it did. . . . The question as to whether a teacher may have

freedom to teach the ordinary principles of science as they are everywhere recognized by educators was not a matter to be settled in a country court and before a partisan judge and jury.[11]

The reactions to the attorneys, Bryan and Darrow, were unsparing. Most of the reports were far from complimentary. One religious magazine lashed out at Darrow:

"Mr. Darrow, chief counsel for the defense, is an avowed atheist, whose main purpose in the entire trial was to broadcast his atheism before the American people."[12]

Others took both attorneys to task for their duel in Dayton.

The world's greatest publicity hounds—William Jennings Bryan and Clarence Darrow—have identified themselves with the prosecution and the defense, respectively, . . . as a matter of fact, their motives are identical—each is in it for the personal advertising he can get.[13]

The *Chicago Daily Tribune* described Bryan in these words: "The import of the Tennessee trial is in the presence of Mr. Bryan there. He represents the real seriousness, not of the act itself but of the pressure behind the act, of the motive and intent in the rear . . . he is shrewd."[14]

Still other media addressed the issue of evolution and the trial's impact on the controversy it presented. A religious monthly magazine sharpened the challenge:

. . . let us organize to boycott every school, editor's chair, and pulpit that sanctions the same (evolutionary teaching) . . . . This fight must be carried into every corner of the country and into politics as well as into religion and education.[15]

Other accounts supported those who believed in evolution and in God. "But there are millions who though their minds give support to the evolutionary theory have also a belief in Divine Creation and a faith with a foundation as firm as that of the pious prosecutors in this case."[16]

Even the media differed about the real value of the *Scopes* story. One said,

> The press has made this story . . . and yet the newspaper workers at the spot warmly disagree as to the 'value' of the story. Some say there is little real public interest in the case. Others consider it the most significant and truly important assignment of their careers.[17]

H. L. Mencken, a reporter for the *Baltimore Sun*, wrote about the trial. The *Sun* newspaper paid part of the defense team's expenses and posted bond for Scopes after his conviction.[18] Naturally the reporting would be biased in favor of the defense. Here are some of the things he wrote about the trial:

About his stay in Dayton:

> I wasted two weeks on the buffoonery, but I think there was some profit in it. For the first time in my life I was in daily contact with Christian people. I got to know dozens of them very well, and have enough material stored up to last me the rest of my life.[19]

About the town of Dayton:

> Two months ago the town was obscure and happy. Today it is a universal joke . . . the town, I confess greatly surprised me. . . . What I found was a country town of charm and even beauty.[20]

About the jury:

> It was obvious after a few rounds that the jury would be unanimously hot for Genesis . . . a panel man who confessed that he was prejudiced against evolution got a hearty round of applause from the crowd.[21]

About the attorneys:

> *William Jennings Bryan:* "He could never be the peasants' President, but there is still a chance to be the peasants' Pope."

> *Clarence Darrow:* The net effect of Clarence Darrow's great speech . . . seems to be precisely the same as if he had bawled it up a rainspout in the interior of Afghanistan. Darrow has lost this case. It was lost long before he came to Dayton. But it seems to me that he has nevertheless performed a great public service by fighting it to a finish.[22]

What Happened to Scopes and Others

John Scopes never did return to the classroom. He accepted funds that several expert witnesses had collected for him, and he enrolled in the University of Chicago. Scopes was somewhat shy and chose not to attend any of the hearings on his case in the Tennessee Supreme Court. After graduation with a degree in geology, Scopes worked for an oil company in Venezuela and Louisiana. He wrote a book, *Center of the Storm*, that detailed his experience in the trial. Scopes died in 1970, three years after the Butler Act was overturned.

On July 26, 1925, only five days after the trial ended, William Jennings Bryan died in Dayton, Tennessee. Bryan

University, named in his honor, was founded in Dayton, Tennessee, as a Christian liberal arts college.

Clarence Darrow's involvement in the case met with harsh criticism from many sources. It was something Darrow had become accustomed to. Even the American Civil Liberties Union hesitated about his involvement. Darrow died in 1938 and is remembered as one of the finest defense attorneys of all time. He represented unpopular clients and causes, opposed the death penalty, and supported First Amendment freedoms.

The flag flies at half mast on Main Street and Market Street in Dayton, marking the death of William Jennings Bryan on July 26, 1925, only five days after the trial ended.

George Rappleyea, the original promoter of the trial, left Dayton for industrial ventures in Cuba, Canada, Alabama, and Florida.[23] F. E. Robinson remained in Dayton as owner of Robinson's Drugstore. Prosecuting attorney Thomas Stewart went on to an impressive career and was elected to the United States Senate from Tennessee in 1942. Governor Austin Peay, who signed the Butler Act into law, was reelected in Tennessee. John Raulston failed to be reelected as judge.[24]

Reaction of the Schools

One year after the *Scopes* trial, George W. Hunter wrote a new science book entitled *A New Civic Biology*. He was careful not to even mention the word *evolution*.[25]

Between the 1920s and early 1960s, biology textbooks avoided the topic of evolution and did not mention the name of Darwin. The coverage of evolution was greatly understated.[26] Although few states passed antievolution bills, widespread antievolution sentiments existed in this country. "In the five years following the *Scopes* trial, state lawmakers considered twenty anti-evolution bills but passed only two into law. Then, for about thirty years, the public controversy over evolution was quiet."[27]

Reaction of the Arts

In 1960, Dayton, Tennessee, hosted the opening of the world premiere of the movie *Inherit the Wind*, which was based on a play by the same name. Although the events of the *Scopes* trial inspired this production, the account was fictionalized and differed in several ways from the trial. The play still has successful runs.

A Turn of Events—The 1960s

In 1967, Tennessee repealed (overturned) its Butler Act. A similar law in an adjoining state, Arkansas, was also about to fall. On November 12, 1968, the United States Supreme Court ruled the Arkansas antievolution law unconstitutional. Four years earlier, in 1964, Susan Epperson, a high school biology teacher in the Little Rock, Arkansas, public schools, had challenged the Arkansas law that made it unlawful for a teacher in any state-supported school to teach that people came from a lower order of animals, or to use a textbook that taught that theory. Violation of the law was a misdemeanor, and violators were subject to dismissal from their teaching positions.[28] Epperson asked the Chancery Court of Arkansas to find the law unconstitutional and to stop the school district from dismissing her from her teaching position.[29]

Although the Arkansas law was worded differently from Tennessee's Butler Act, the United States Supreme Court concluded that the Arkansas law was similar to the famous 1925 Tennessee "monkey law" and declared the law unconstitutional.[30]

This Court said the law interfered with freedom of speech granted in the First Amendment, and would "hinder the quest for knowledge, restrict the freedom to learn, and restrain the freedom to teach."[31]

On appeal, the Supreme Court of Arkansas reversed the lower court's decision and wrote a short two-sentence

chapter ten

THE IMPACT OF THE *SCOPES* TRIAL

AFTERMATH—During the 1950s, the Soviet Union launched a satellite into space, beating the United States in the "race to space." The National Science Foundation in the United States became concerned that American students were following behind the students in other countries. Several programs were designed to bring the teaching of science up-to-date in schools in the United States. The theory of evolution was also added to biology books.[1]

The 1960s

As a result, in the early 1960s, certain religious groups raised concerns about a loss of traditional values. These groups spoke out against the teaching of evolution and introduced a theory called creation science.[2] The theory of creation science claimed that the universe and life in it came about suddenly and from nothing. Those who supported this theory argued that Darwin's view that all living things came from a single organism was insufficient. Followers of creation science supported these ideas:

1. Changes occur only within fixed limits of the plant and animal kingdoms.

2. Humans and apes have separate ancestries.

3. The earth's geology was created by sudden and violent events, one of which was a worldwide flood.

4. The earth and all life are recent creations.[3]

The 1970s

In the 1960s and early 1970s, several organizations promoted the idea that scientific evidence supported the Creation account found in the Bible. The Institute for Creation Research (ICR) of San Diego became the leader of the movement. Creation Life Publishing Company published creation science material. In 1963, a breakaway group from the American Scientific Affiliation founded the Creation Research Society (CRS) and declared its purpose was "to reach all people with the vital message of the scientific and historic truth about creation." In 1970, a group known as the CSRC separated from the CRS. Its mission was to "reach the 63 million children of the United States with the scientific teaching of Biblical creationism."[4]

The 1980s

By the 1980s, the promoters of creation science, had influenced lawmakers in Arkansas and Louisiana. Both states passed laws that required teachers to present a balanced treatment of creation science *and* evolution.

"The Balanced Treatment for Creation-Science and Evolution-Science Act" became law in Arkansas on March 19, 1981.[5] Less than two-and-one-half months after the law was passed, on May 27, 1981, a lawsuit was filed challenging the validity of the law.

McLean v. *Arkansas Board of Education*

Those challenging the validity of the balanced treatment law argued that the law was invalid on three grounds:

1. It established a religion.

2. It violated academic freedom of students and teachers.

3. It was vague.[6]

The United States Supreme Court, on January 5, 1982, declared the Arkansas law unconstitutional. In the Supreme Court's view, the "evidence is overwhelming that both the purpose and effect of Act 590 is the advancement of religion in the public schools."[7] The Court ruled that creation science lacked educational value and was not a science.[8] The Supreme Court's decision said the theory of creation science depended on faith for its interpretation.[9] All Justices on the Court agreed that the Arkansas law was unconstitutional.

The Supreme Court wrote about the testimony of Marianne Wilson who was in charge of the science curriculum for Pulaski County Special School District, the largest school district in the state of Arkansas. After the balanced-treatment law was passed in Arkansas, Wilson was asked to produce a creation science curriculum for the Pulaski County Special School District. She worked with a committee of science teachers, and approached the assignment with no bias either way. Wilson and her committee reviewed practically all the creationist material. They unanimously agreed to report to the school board that creationism was not a science but a religion. "The board ignored Ms. Wilson's recommendation and insisted that a curriculum guide be prepared."[10]

In considering the case, the Supreme Court concluded, "There is no way teachers can teach the Genesis account of Creation in a secular manner."[11] A permanent injunction, a court order that prohibited the school from using the creation science material, was granted. Since the purpose of creation science was to advance a particular religious belief, requiring that it be taught in the public schools made the law unconstitutional.[12]

Edwards v. *Aguillard*

On June 10, 1987, *Edwards* v. *Aguillard* came before the Justices of the United States Supreme Court.[13] The case challenged the constitutionality of a law known as the Louisiana Balanced Treatment for Creation Science and Evolution Science in Public School Instruction Act.[14]

The Majority Opinion. Justice William Brennan wrote the opinion of the majority of the Justices on the Court. It stated that the Louisiana law served no secular purpose, and "has as its primary purpose the promotion of a particular religious belief and is thus unconstitutional."[15]

The Louisiana law required a teacher in public elementary and secondary schools who taught evolution science to also teach the theory of creation science. There was no requirement that evolution be taught. If it were taught, however, then creation science would have to be given a balanced share of time. Parents of children in the Louisiana public schools, Louisiana teachers, and religious leaders challenged the law in the courts.

The federal district court held that the law violated the Establishment Clause of the First Amendment, and said the law was "unconstitutional." Those who lost at the federal district court level appealed to the United States Supreme Court.

The majority of the Justices on the Supreme Court agreed with the federal district court decision. The Supreme Court's decision stated:

> Families entrust public schools with the education of their children, but condition their trust on the understanding that the classroom will not purposely be used to advance religious views that may conflict with the private beliefs of the student and his or her family. Students in such institutions are impressionable and their attendance is involuntary.[16]

The majority of the Justices decided the law was unconstitutional. They used a test known as the *Lemon* test to determine whether the law violated the First Amendment. That test came from a case known as *Lemon* v. *Kurtzman*, in which three questions were asked to determine whether a law was constitutional:

1. Does the law have a secular purpose?

2. Does the law advance or inhibit religion?

3. Does the law result in excessive entanglement with religion?[17]

The Court's majority said, "The preeminent purpose of the Louisiana Legislature was clearly to advance the religious viewpoint that a supernatural being created humankind." An expert who had testified before Louisiana lawmakers admitted, "The theory of creation science included belief in the existence of a supernatural creator."[18]

The Minority Dissent. Unlike the *McLean* case, in which all the Justices agreed with the decision, this time the Court was divided in its opinion. Justice Antonin Scalia filed a dissent, and Justice William Rehnquist joined in that dissent.

Justice Scalia wrote that creation science was a scientific theory, and that the "plain meaning of the term creation is not necessarily religious."[19] Scalia, in his dissent, warned that "striking down a law approved by the democratically elected representatives of the people is no minor matter."[20]

Evolutionists claimed a victory in the decision in *Edwards* v. *Aguillard*. The twenty-three bills requiring equal time for creation science in fifteen states were all but finished. But some predicted the long-standing battle with those who supported the fundamentalist movement would probably continue.[21]

The 1990s

In the 1990s, a strong wall of separation between church and state was evident in our schools. Many citizens believed that such protection was necessary in American schools where students of many different religious beliefs gathered.

Although antievolutionists had lost their "day in court," their presence was known. Eight states avoided all mention of evolution in their schools. Alabama used a disclaimer about evolution in its textbooks. Kansas removed the theory of evolution from its standardized tests, all but ensuring it would not be taught in classrooms. All but fourteen states reported controversies surrounding this issue in the public schools, according to the National Center for Science Education.[22] "Evolution-creation controversy is as charged today as it was when Scopes was tried," Randy Moore, a biology professor, recently said. "Creationists are more powerful than ever. They're winning, not in terms of court cases, but what happens in classrooms. I get three to five phone calls a week from teachers with problems."[23]

Educators and publishers of textbooks are as careful today as they may have been in 1925. In order to avoid problems, publishers may leave out chapters that deal with the creation of the earth when shipping textbooks to certain states. Some schools may glue together offending pages. The Alabama State Board of Education approved a 260-word insert for its textbooks that states any statement about life's origins should be considered as theory, not fact. Under pressure, Macmillan-McGraw Hill publishers printed a new version of its *Changing Earth* textbook to exclude a chapter on the earth's age.[24]

Some scientists continue to question the theory of evolution. In *Darwin's Black Box*, biochemist Michael Behe challenged Darwin's theory of evolution. The author claimed that we can understand how something works but not necessarily how it came to be. He also claimed evolution means different things to different people and that the cell is no longer the mysterious black box that it was for Darwin. Behe claimed the complex structure of the cell depends on far too many interconnected parts to have been built up gradually, step by tiny step, over time.[25]

Science journalist Richard Milton also challenged Darwin's theories. He claimed there are "missing links" in every evolutionary line, human and otherwise. He also claimed that even if the evolutionary process occurred over the course of 3.8 billion years, that would not be long enough for complex life to evolve from single-celled organisms. He concluded that to believe in Darwinism requires more of an act of faith than does a functioning science.[26]

The National Academy of Sciences, perhaps the nation's leading scientific organization, claimed that "evolution must be a vital part of science instruction, and lessons on creationism do not belong in science classes." The Academy also said, "Evolution is supported by overwhelming evidence." In spite of favorable court decisions, the organization is concerned that there are widespread misunderstandings about evolution and that teachers are

The Scopes *trial was held in Rhea County Courthouse in Dayton, Tennessee, from July 10 through July 21, 1925. Today, this renovated historic building houses a* Scopes Trial Museum. *Each year in July the members of the town reenact a shortened version of the trial for the public.*

reluctant to teach the theory in classrooms today. As concerns rise, this organization has produced a guidebook, *Teaching About Evolution and the Nature of Science*, to help educators integrate lessons about evolution in basic biology for children beginning in kindergarten. "Teaching evolution is essential for explaining some of the most fundamental concepts of science," the guide states.[27]

Don Aguillard, a Louisiana science teacher who took his case to the United States Supreme Court, warned that "the battle goes on, and the task has shifted from constitutional challenges to grass-roots efforts."[28] Even if antievolutionists are not successful in the courts, their challenges are made known in other ways. For example, a recent survey found that approximately 45 percent of twelve hundred first-year students in ten different colleges rejected the theory of evolution.[29]

On August 13, 1999, the Fifth Circuit Court of Appeals handed down a decision in the case of *Freiler* v. *Tangipahoa Board of Education*, affirming a lower court decision. The court found that the primary effect of requiring a teacher to read out loud a certain disclaimer whenever evolution was taught, protected and maintained a particular religious viewpoint, namely belief in the biblical version of Creation, and was therefore unconstitutional.

On December 7, 1999, the Kansas State Board of Education adopted curriculum standards for science education that deleted all references to the origins and evolution of the universe. This action captured headlines and stirred a renewed interest in what part evolution should play in science graduation standards. The debate goes on.

The trial of John Thomas Scopes may have ended on July 21, 1925, but the issues are still being discussed today. When values and beliefs are threatened, especially if those beliefs are religious ones, people will continue to respond with the same passion and fervor as did those who came to Dayton, Tennessee, in 1925.

The United States of America was founded on First Amendment freedoms. That amendment protects citizens from state-established religion, and also guarantees freedom of speech. What can a teacher say about evolution? What, if anything, can a science teacher say about the book of Genesis? Do students have a right to be introduced to all theories of creation even if one of those theories is based on a religious belief? These questions and others like them are asked in classrooms all over this country.

The tensions that gave the *Scopes* trial worldwide recognition continue to raise questions some seventy-five years later, and these questions have no easy answers. We can be assured that in this new century the voices of the *Scopes* trial will continue to be heard. It remains for each generation to struggle with a way to achieve a balance of freedom of speech and freedom of religion within the spirit and meaning of the First Amendment.

Chronology

November 24, 1859—Charles Darwin's *Origin of Species* is published in England.

August 3, 1900—John Thomas Scopes is born in Paducah, Kentucky.

March 21, 1925—Butler Act becomes law in Tennessee.

April 24, 1925—John Scopes teaches evolution in a Dayton, Tennessee, high school biology class.

May 25, 1925—John Scopes is indicted by Tennessee grand jury to stand trial for teaching evolution in the public schools.

July 10–21, 1925—Dayton, Tennessee, hosts the *State of Tennessee* v. *John Scopes* trial ending in conviction of John Scopes.

January 17, 1927—Tennessee Supreme Court reverses *State of Tennessee* v. *John Scopes* conviction on a technicality.

September 1, 1967—Tennessee's Butler Act is repealed.

November 12, 1968—United States Supreme Court rules in *Epperson* v. *Arkansas* that Arkansas's antievolution law is unconstitutional.

January 5, 1982—United States Supreme Court rules in *McLean* v. *Arkansas Board of Education* that Arkansas law requiring balanced treatment of teaching creation science and evolution science is unconstitutional.

June 19, 1987—United States Supreme Court rules in *Edwards* v. *Aguillard* that Louisiana's balanced treatment of creation science and evolution science law is unconstitutional. The Court found that the law's primary purpose was to promote a particular religious belief.

August 13, 1999—Fifth Circuit Court of Appeals rules in *Freiler* v. *Tangipahoa* that it is unconstitutional to require a teacher to read a disclaimer whenever evolution is taught.

December 7, 1999—Kansas State Board of Education adopts curriculum standards for science education that delete references to the origins and evolution of the universe.

Chapter Notes

Chapter 1. A Court or a Circus?

1. Chapter 27, Laws of Tennessee, March 21, 1925, Butler Act.

2. United States Constitution, First Amendment, December 15, 1791.

Chapter 2. Darwin and the Fundamentalists

1. Charles Darwin, *The Autobiography of Charles Darwin,* Francis Darwin, ed. (New York: Dover Publications, Inc., 1892), pp. 218–220.

2. Ibid., p. 225.

3. Ibid., p. 453.

4. George William Hunter, *A Civic Biology* (New York: American Book Company, 1914), pp. 194–196.

5. George Wright, "The Passing of Evolution," *The Fundamentals*, undated, vol. 7, p. 20.

6. "Evolutionism in the Pulpit," reprinted from Herald and Presbyter, *The Fundamentals*, undated, vol. 8, p. 30.

7. Henry H. Beach, "Decadence of Darwinism," *The Fundamentals*, 1912, vol. 8, p. 48.

8. UMKC Law, *Scopes* Trial Home Page, *State* v. *John Scopes*, © 1997, <http://www.law.umkc.edu/faculty/projects/ftrials/scopes> (September 24, 1999).

9. Edward J. Larsen, *Summer for the Gods* (New York: Perseus Books, 1997), p. 43.

10. Ibid., p. 48.

11. UMKC Law, *Scopes* Trial Home Page, <http://www.law.umkc.edu/faculty/ftrials/scopes>.

12. Ibid.

Chapter 3. Robinson's Drugstore

1. Sprague de Camp, *The Great Monkey Trial* (Garden City, N.Y.: Doubleday and Company, 1968), p. 8.

2. ACLU Briefing Paper Number 1, American Civil Liberties Union home page, © 1999 <http://www.aclu.org> (September 24, 1999).

3. Ibid.

4. UMKC Law, *Scopes* Trial Home Page, "Dayton, Tennessee," © 1997, <http://www.law.umkc.edu/faculty/projects/ftrials/scopes> (September 24, 1999).

5. Richard M. Cornelius, *World's Most Famous Court Trial*, reprinted with permission from *History of Rhea County, Tennessee*, compiled by Bettye J. Broyles (Rhea County, Tenn: Rhea County Historical and Genealogical Society, 1991), p. 67.

6. Scopes, p. 53.

7. Ibid.

8. de Camp, pp. 11–13.

Chapter 4. John Scopes and the Antievolution Act

1. John Scopes, *Center of the Storm* (New York: Holt, Rinehart and Winston, 1967), p. 44.

2. Ibid., p. 56.

3. Ibid., p. 57.

4. Lee Arbetman and Richard L. Roe, *Great Trials in American History: Civil War to the Present* (St. Paul, Minn.: West Publishing Co., 1985), p. 25.

5. UMKC Law, *Scopes* Trial Home Page, © 1997, <http://www.law.umkc.edu/faculty/projects/ftrials/scopes> (September 25, 1999).

6. Scopes, p. 53.

7. Kevin Tierney, *Darrow: A Biography* (New York: Thomas Y. Crowell Publishers, 1979), p. 362.

8. Scopes, pp. 72–73.

Chapter 5. Two Attorneys Clash

1. Richard Cornelius, *William Jennings Bryan: The Scopes*

Trial and Inherit the Wind (Dayton, Tenn.: Bryan College Press, 1997), pp. 1–2.

    2. Ibid., p. 2.

    3. Ibid.

    4. Kevin Tierney, *Darrow: A Biography* (New York: Thomas Y. Crowell Publishers, 1979), p. 360.

    5. Elmer Gertz, "Clarence Darrow: Legendary Lawyer of American History," *Caxtonian* 6, no. 3, March 1998, p. 1.

    6. Clarence Darrow, *The Story of My Life* (New York: Charles Scribner's Sons, 1932), p. 249.

    7. Tierney, p. 362.

    8. Arthur and Lila Weinberg, *Clarence Darrow: A Sentimental Rebel* (New York: G. P. Putnam's Sons, 1980), p. 319.

    9. Ibid., pp. 320–321.

    10. Irving Stone, *Clarence Darrow for the Defense* (Garden City, N.Y.: Doubleday & Company, Inc.,), p. 431.

    11. Ibid., p. 436.

    12. Tom McGowan, *The Great Monkey Trial: Science vs. Fundamentalism in America* (New York: Oxford University Press, 1990), p. 63.

    13. Stone, p. 444–445.

    14. Ibid., p. 356.

Chapter 6. Judge and Jury

    1. Edward J. Larsen, *Summer for the Gods* (New York: Perseus Books, 1997), p. 109.

    2. Sheldon Norman Grebstein, ed., *Monkey Trial* (Boston: Houghton Mifflin Company, 1960), p. 35.

    3. Ray Ginger, *Six Days or Forever?* (Oxford, England: Oxford University Press, 1958), p. 95.

    4. Ibid., p. 96

    5. Larsen, p. 153.

    6. John Scopes, *World's Most Famous Court Trial: State of Tennessee vs. John T. Scopes* (New York: Da Capo Press, Inc., 1971), p. 67.

7. Sterling Tracy, "No Modernists Named in Scopes Jury: All Believe in Bible," *Commercial Appeal* (Memphis, Tenn.), July 11, 1925, p. 1.

8. Ginger, p. 93.

9. UMKC Law, *Scopes* Trial Home Page, © 1997, <http://www.law.umkc.edu/faculty/projects/ftrials/scopes> (September 24, 1999).

10. Ibid.

11. Ginger, p. 111.

12. Ibid., p. 104.

13. Larsen, p. 168.

14. Ibid., p. 148.

15. Original transcript of the *Scopes* v. *Tennessee* Case (Cincinnati, Ohio: National Book Company, 1925), pp. 111–112, reprinted by The Notable Trials Library, Alan M. Dershowitz, chairman (New York: Gryphon Editions, 1990).

16. Larsen, p. 150.

17. Richard M. Cornelius, *The Trial That Is Still Being Tried: The Scopes Evolution Trial* (Dayton, Tenn.: Dayton College Press, 1998), p. 3.

Chapter 7. The Case for Tennessee

1. Original transcript of the *Scopes* v. *Tennessee* Case (Cincinnati, Ohio: National Book Company, 1925), p. 170, reprinted by The Notable Trials Library, Alan M. Dershowitz, chairman (New York: Gryphon Editions, 1990).

2. UMKC Law, The *Scopes* Trial Home Page, © 1997, <http://www.law.umkc.edu/faculty/projects/ftrials/scopes> (September 24, 1999).

3. Original transcript *Scopes* v. *Tennessee*, p. 150.

4. *Scopes* Trial Home Page.

5. Original transcript *Scopes* v. *Tennessee*, p. 170.

6. Ibid., p. 171.

7. Ibid.

8. Richard Cornelius, "The Trial That Made Monkeys out of the World," *USA Today*, November 1990, p. 90.

9. Sheldon Norman Grebstein, ed., *Monkey Trial* (Boston: Houghton Mifflin Company, 1960), p. 96.

10. Original transcript *Scopes* v. *Tennessee*, p. 122.

11. Ibid., p. 123.

12. Grebstein, p. 99.

13. Original transcript *Scopes* v. *Tennessee*, p. 126.

14. *Scopes* Trial Home Page, "Trial Excerpts," p. 9.

15. Original transcript *Scopes* v. *Tennessee*, p. 129.

16. Ibid.

17. Grebstein, p. 108.

18. Ibid.

19. Ibid., p. 109.

Chapter 8. The Case for John Scopes

1. *Tinker* v. *Des Moines School District*, 393 U.S. 503, 71, 72 (1969).

2. Original transcript of the *Scopes* v. *Tennessee* Case (Cincinnati, Ohio: National Book Company, 1925), p. 171, reprinted by The Notable Trials Library, Alan M. Dershowitz, chairman (New York: Gryphon Editions, 1990).

3. UMKC Law, *Scopes* Trial Home Page, © 1997, <http:// www.law.umkc.edu/faculty/projects/ftrials/scopes> (September 24, 1999).

4. Ibid.

5. Original transcript *Scopes* v. *Tennessee*, p. 115.

6. Ibid., pp. 116–117.

7. Leslie H. Allen, ed., *Bryan and Darrow at Dayton* (New York: Russell & Russell, 1925), pp. 126–127.

8. Original transcript *Scopes* v. *Tennessee*, p. 229.

9. Ibid.

10. *Scopes* Trial Home Page, "The Defense Experts," p. 1.

11. Original transcript *Scopes* v. *Tennessee*, pp. 234–238.

12. Allen, p. 130.

13. Original transcript *Scopes* v. *Tennessee*, p. 241.

14. Ibid., p. 249.

15. Allen, p. 130.

16. Original transcript *Scopes* v. *Tennessee*, pp. 275–279.

17. Sheldon Norman Grebstein, ed., *Monkey Trial* (Boston: Houghton Mifflin Company, 1960), p. 110.

18. Ibid.

19. Original transcript *Scopes* v. *Tennessee*, p. 138.

20. Ibid.

21. Grebstein, p. 114.

22. Original transcript *Scopes* v. *Tennessee*, p. 155.

23. Ibid., p. 176.

24. Ibid., p. 182.

25. Ibid., pp. 187–188.

26. Ibid., p. 170.

27. Grebstein, p. 143.

28. Original transcript *Scopes* v. *Tennessee*, p. 207.

29. Ibid., p. 225.

30. Ibid., p. 226.

31. Grebstein, p. 144.

32. Allen, pp. 150–151.

33. Sprague de Camp, *The Great Monkey Trial* (Garden City, N.Y.: Doubleday & Company, 1968), p. 403.

34. Ibid.

35. Original transcript *Scopes* v. *Tennessee*, p. 299.

36. Ibid.

37. Ibid.

38. Ibid., p. 304.

Chapter 9. The Jury Decides

1. Original transcript of the *Scopes* v. *Tennessee Case* (Cincinnati, Ohio: National Book Company, 1925), p. 306, reprinted by The Notable Trials Library, Alan M. Dershowitz, chairman (New York: Gryphon Editions, 1990).

2. Ibid., pp. 309–311.

3. Ibid., p. 312.

4. Ibid., p. 313.

5. Ibid.

6. Edward J. Larsen, *Summer for the Gods* (New York: Perseus Books, 1997), p. 207.

7. *Scopes* v. *State of Tennessee*, 154 Tenn. 105, 289 SW 367 (Tenn. 1927).

8. "Jury Returns Verdict of 'Guilty' in Scopes Case," *The Dayton Herald* (Dayton, Tenn.), July 23, 1925, p. 1.

9. "The Scopes Trial," *The Atlanta Constitution*, July 22, 1925, p. 6.

10. "Dayton Relapses," *The Manchester Guardian Weekly* (Manchester, England), July 24, 1925, p. 61.

11. "Amateur Dramatics at Dayton," *The Christian Century*, July 30, 1925, p. 969.

12. "The Scopes Trial," *The Baptist Monthly Magazine*, August 1925, p. 10.

13. "Faith and Evolution," *The Los Angeles Times*, July 14, 1925, p. 4.

14. "The *Scopes* Trial," *The Chicago Daily Tribune*, July 17, 1925, p. 8.

15. Thomas H. Nelson, "The Real Issue in Tennessee," *The Moody Bible Institute Monthly*, September 1925, p. 11.

16. "The Unity of Knowledge," *The New York Times*, July 19, 1925, p. 6.

17. Michael Williams, "At Dayton, Tennessee," *The Commonwealth*, July 22, 1925, p. 262.

18. UMKC Law, *Scopes* Trial Home Page, H. L. Mencken Account, "The Monkey Trial," © 1997, <http://www.law.umkc.edu/faculty/projects/ftrials/scopes> (September 24, 1999).

19. H. L. Mencken, *Twenty-five Years of Newspaper Work* (Baltimore, Md.: Johns Hopkins University Press, 1994), p. 149.

20. *Scopes* Trial Home Page, p. 1.

21. Ibid., pp. 1–2.

22. Ibid., pp. 1–4.

23. Richard M. Cornelius, *World's Most Famous Court Trial*, reprinted with permission from *History of Rhea County, Tennessee*, compiled by Bettye J. Broyles (Rhea County, Tenn: Rhea County Historical and Genealogical Society, 1991), p. 67.

24. Ibid., p. 70.

25. Ibid.

26. *McLean* v. *Arkansas Board of Education*, 525 F. Supp. 1259 (1982).

27. Richard Cornelius, "The Trial That Made Monkeys Out of the World," *USA Today*, November 1990, p. 90.

28. *Epperson* v. *Arkansas*, 393 U.S. 98, 99 (1968).

29. Ibid., p. 100.

30. Ibid., p. 98.

31. Ibid.

32. Ibid., p. 101.

33. Ibid.

34. Ibid., p. 109.

35. Ibid., pp. 113–114.

36. Ibid., pp. 115–116.

Chapter 10. The Impact of the *Scopes* Trial

1. *McLean* v. *Arkansas Board of Education*, 525 F. Supp. 1259 (1982).

2. Ibid.

3. Ibid., p. 1264.

4. Ibid., pp. 1259–1260.

5. Arkansas Law, Section 80-1663, 1981.

6. *McLean* v. *Arkansas Board of Education*, p. 1257.

7. Ibid., p. 1264.

8. Ibid., p. 1267.

9. Ibid., p. 1269.

10. Ibid., p. 1270.

11. Ibid., p. 1271.

12. Ibid., p. 1255.

13. *Edwards* v. *Aguillard*, 107 S. Ct. 2573 (1987).

14. LSA-R.S. 17-286.1-17.186.7 (Louisiana).

15. *Edwards* v. *Aguillard*, p. 2574.

16. Ibid., p. 2577.

17. *Lemon* v. *Kurtzman*, 403 U.S. 602, 612, 613, 91 S. Ct. 2105, 2111 (1971).

18. *Edwards* v. *Aguillard*, p. 2581.

19. Ibid., p. 2602.

20. Ibid., p. 2600.

21. Sharon Williams, "The United States Supreme Court Denies Equal Time for Scientific Creationism in the Public Schools—Scopes in Reverse?" *UMKC Law Review*, vol. 56, no. 3, 1988, p. 615.

22. Jon Christensen, "Teachers Fight for Darwin's Place in U.S. Classrooms," *The New York Times*, November 24, 1998, p. F3.

23. Ibid.

24. Larry Witham, "School Boards Challenge Textbooks With Evolution Big Bang Theories," *Insight on the News*, vol. 13, no. 4, February 3, 1997, p. 4.

25. Tom Woodward, "Meeting Darwin's Wager," *Christianity Today*, April 28, 1997, p. 16.; Michael J. Behe, *Darwin's Black Box* (New York: Simon & Schuster, 1996), pp. ix, x.

26. Richard Milton, *Shattering the Myths of Darwinism* (Rochester, Vt.: Park Street Press, 1997), back cover.

27. "Evolution Must Be Taught If Students Are to Understand Modern Biology," *Skeptical Inquirer*, July–August 1998, p. 5.

28. Christensen, p. F3.

29. "What Are They Thinking? Science Education News and Analysis," *Scientific American*, October, 1997, p. 34.

Glossary

agnostic—A person who doubts the existence of God.

appeal—The process of bringing a case to a higher court for a decision. John Scopes appealed his conviction to the Tennessee Supreme Court.

atheist—A person who denies the existence of God.

balanced treatment—The result of laws passed in Arkansas and Louisiana that required the teaching of creationism when evolutionary theory was taught. The United States Supreme Court declared these laws unconstitutional in *McLean* v. *Arkansas Board of Education* and *Edwards* v. *Aguillard*.

beyond a reasonable doubt—The standard of proof needed in a criminal trial in order to find a defendant guilty of a crime. The facts must fully convince the juror of the defendant's guilt.

Bill of Rights—The first ten amendments to the United States Constitution. It guarantees certain freedoms.

Butler Act—A Tennessee law passed on March 21, 1925. It prohibited the teaching of evolution in the public schools of Tennessee.

conviction—A decision by a judge or jury that the defendant committed the crime.

creationism—A theory that supports the biblical account

found in the book of Genesis about how the world was created.

creation science—Scientific evidence or arguments put forth in support of the biblical account of how the world was created.

cross-examination—The questioning of an opposing witness in a trial. The process serves to test the validity of a witness's testimony.

defendant—The one accused of a crime in a trial.

direct-examination—The questioning of one's own witness in a trial. The process serves to establish the case based on the evidence presented.

evidence—The testimony, records, documents, or objects introduced in a trial that serve to convince a jury or the court of the facts of the case.

evolution—A theory written in 1859 in which Charles Darwin claimed that all life evolved from a single organism.

expert witness—A person qualified to give testimony in a case because of education or special knowledge. The expert witnesses brought to the *Scopes* trial were not allowed to give testimony because the judge ruled the testimony inadmissible.

felony—A very serious crime punishable by fine and imprisonment for at least one year. Murder, burglary, and rape are examples of felony crimes.

First Amendment—The part of the Bill of Rights that protects freedom of religion and speech, but also restricts the government from favoring a particular religious belief.

Fourteenth Amendment—This addition to the United States Constitution required not only the federal government but also each state to give its citizens the rights protected in the Bill of Rights.

fundamentalism—A religious movement that maintained certain basic Christian beliefs. Followers oppose the teaching of Darwin's theory of evolution in the public schools and many of them encourage state lawmakers to pass laws prohibiting its teaching.

grand jury—A jury that hears evidence presented on behalf of the state, and based on that evidence determines whether a trial should be held.

inadmissible—In a trial, certain evidence or testimony that the judge rules is not allowed to be included.

indictment—A formal, written charge of a crime. It signifies the fact that sufficient evidence exists to bring a person to trial for a particular crime. Usually indictments involve serious crimes, but in this case, John Scopes was indicted of a misdemeanor.

jury—Twelve people (in the *Scopes* case, all men) chosen from a panel of men and women. They determine whether the defendant has committed the crime "beyond a reasonable doubt." The jury took only nine minutes to find John T. Scopes guilty of teaching evolution, in violation of the Butler Act.

media—Coverage of news. The *Scopes* trial marked the first radio broadcast of an American trial. Newspaper reporters and telegraph operators reported on the trial as well.

misdemeanor—A lesser crime than a felony. John Scopes was found guilty of a misdemeanor violation that resulted in a fine of one hundred dollars.

modernism—A religious viewpoint that accepted modern thinking. Modernists accepted both the theory of evolution and the biblical account of Creation in Genesis.

Monkey Laws—The name given to laws that prohibited the teaching of evolutionary theory in the classroom.

nolle prosequi—A Latin term meaning not to prosecute further, or to "drop the case" against the defendant.

plaintiff—The person who brings a charge of a crime against another person.

prosecute—To charge and present evidence in a court stating that the defendant has committed a crime.

reversal—To change a court's decision by appeal to a higher court. The Tennessee Supreme Court reversed the *Scopes* decision, and suggested that the case not be prosecuted further.

theory—An idea based on principles or knowledge that is speculative. The theory of evolution was disputed in the *Scopes* trial.

trial—A criminal proceeding in which witnesses give testimony, and a decision is made about the guilt or innocence of the defendant.

unconstitutional law—A law that goes against the United States Constitution. The Butler Act was repealed (taken off the books) in 1967 before the United States Supreme Court found that a similar Arkansas antievolution law violated the First Amendment's provision for separation of church and state.

United States Supreme Court—The highest court in the United States, comprised of nine lifetime Justices who are appointed by the president. The Justices make decisions that become the final law of the land. The Supreme Court never did decide the *Scopes* case.

Further Reading

Blake, Arthur. *The Scopes Trial: Defending the Right to Teach.* Brookfield, Conn.: Millbrook Press, 1994.

Cornelius, R. M. *Scopes: Creation on Trial.* Green Forest, Ark.: Master Books, 1999.

Driemen, John Evans. *Clarence Darrow.* New York: Chelsea House Publishers, 1992.

Nardo, Don. *The Scopes Trial.* San Diego: Lucent Books, 1997.

Smout, Kary D. *The Creation Evolution Controversy: A Battle for Cultural Power.* Westport, Conn.: Greenwood Publishing Group, Inc., 1998.

Thorndike, Jonathan L. *Epperson v. Arkansas: The Evolution–Creationism Debate.* Springfield, N.J.: Enslow Publishers, Inc., 1999.

Internet Addresses

Charles Darwin

<http://www.turnpike.net/~mscott/darwin.htm>

Charles Darwin—Voyage of the Beagle

<http://www.biology.com/visitors/ae/voyage/
introduction.html>

**Brief History of the Evolution and
Creation Science Conflict**

<http://www.religioustolerance.org/evolutio.htm>

University of Missouri, Kansas City
Scopes **Trial Home Page**

<http://www.law.umkc.edu/faculty/projects/ftrials/
scopes/scopes.htm>

Index